WILLIAM GREENLEAF ELIOT
CONSERVATIVE RADICAL

Plaque in Eliot Hall, First Unitarian Church
(Courtesy Washington University Archives)

WILLIAM GREENLEAF ELIOT
CONSERVATIVE RADICAL

Six essays on the life and character of the

19th Century Unitarian minister, educator and

philanthropist, based on the 1983 Minns Lectures

by

Earl K. Holt III, Minister

First Unitarian Church of St. Louis

With an additional essay on Eliot's early life by

William A. Deiss, Deputy Archivist

Smithsonian Institution Archives

Published by the First Unitarian Church of St. Louis, on the occasion of the 150th Anniversary of its founding, as the First Congregational Society of St. Louis (the Church of the Messiah), on January 26, 1835.

DEDICATION

This book is dedicated to the people of the First Unitarian Church of St. Louis, who are the spiritual as well as institutional heirs of the Church of Messiah, that they may remember the past with appreciation and look forward to the future with hope. As Dr. Eliot said to the congregation a century ago, "The past has much for which we may reasonably be grateful, but the future must and will have greater things in store."

It is also dedicated in grateful memory to these dear friends, to whom this legacy meant so much:

> Elizabeth C. Carson
> Charles D. DePew, Jr.
> Irma Fulbright
> Edith Gummersheimer

FOREWORD

In the spirit of full disclosure so prized in the 1980s, I confess I am deeply indebted to William Greenleaf Eliot and, hence, have a bias in favor of these essays. In a sense, I am one of Dr. Eliot's heirs, fortunate to serve temporarily in one of the institutions which he and his congregation founded. Washington University in St. Louis evolved from Eliot Seminary and, but for the modesty of the founder, would today be a visible memorial called Eliot University. Thus, I have benefitted even more than most from his ability to provide the vision and inspiration on which great leadership and great accomplishments depend. When Earl K. Holt III, Minister of the First Unitarian Church of St. Louis, another of his heirs in responsibility and in that sense my spiritual relative, decided to write on William Greenleaf Eliot, I was delighted.

My early bias was reinforced when I learned that the essays would deal with the character as well as the life of Dr. Eliot. The character of William Greenleaf Eliot suggests almost automatically his virtues — those traits of character that allowed a frail young minister from Boston to lead the efforts to civilize a frontier town on the Mississippi river and to create in that town enduring institutions to serve its educational, religious and social service needs. He and his parishioners laid the groundwork for what was to be by the year 1900 one of the most dynamic cities in the nation.

In this book Earl Holt offers us the opportunity to become acquainted with this remarkable man from a very different era — a man and an era from which we in the 1980s have much to learn. William Greenleaf Eliot valued duty ahead of influence or fame, disinterested devotion ahead of great talent, self-forgetfulness ahead of self-fulfillment and service ahead of personal gain. We modern Americans usually start with different assumptions and with very different goals. But it is well to remember that our views are not the final truth. Styles of character and virtue change as do fashions in clothes although at a much slower rate. The counter currents to our easy acceptance of a rather comfortable, sophisticated, hedonistic society are already evident. It is a good time to rediscover the virtues of some of the best leaders of the early 19th century and to see, as in the life of Dr. Eliot, that commitment to duty and to great causes can go hand in hand with dedication to tolerance and to religious freedom. I am indebted to Earl Holt for so ably bringing alive again William Greenleaf Eliot and his era.

William H. Danforth
Chancellor
Washington University

AUTHOR'S INTRODUCTION

Ministers should not pretend to be scholars. "My life is all broken in little pieces," William Greenleaf Eliot once wrote in his diary. It is the lament of every parish minister, though it has to be said that the unending variety of the demands upon time and energy is also one of the attractions of what is surely the last generalist profession. But it is no life for the real scholar, whose most important work requires extended periods of that most precious of commodities, time — and sometimes the luxuries of research assistants, secretaries, functioning copying machines, word processors, etc. — which few churches find it possible to provide their preachers.

So look at what you hold in your hand as more a labor of love than a work of scholarship. It reflects uncounted moments — too rarely hours — stolen from parishioners, family, friends.

But it must be admitted that such work is also a distraction from the petty distractions of contemporary life, distractions unknown even to our near ancestors. The productivity not just of an exceptional man like William Eliot but even of the average parish minister of the nineteenth century should humble any of us clergy today who complain about our busy-ness and overcrowded calendars. We have as many hours in our day as they had in theirs, and the fact is that without telephones, without typewriters, without automobiles, they accomplished as much — probably more — than we do today. Life was much less complicated then, we rationalize. But if their world appears simpler to us, I am sure it seemed no simpler to them. And a close look reveals a life as various and complex as most of us know. But there are differences. The distractions were less abundant. Radio, television, mass entertainments and all else that contributes to the noise of our lives did not exist. There was no leisure time industry because there wasn't much leisure time. And they possessed a clarity of purpose which we seem to have lost. At least the best of them did, and to rediscover that is one of particular rewards of time spent reading the journals and letters of an era so different from our own.

*   *   *

I first heard of William Greenleaf Eliot ten years ago, when I was extended a call by the First Unitarian Church of St. Louis. I knew him first as the grandfather of T. S. Eliot, next as the first Minister of the Church I was coming to serve (which had been known as the Church of the Messiah until it merged with another Unitarian congregation, the Church of the Unity, in 1938). As a life-long Unitarian, I knew the Eliot name of course. Two Eliots had served as President of the American Unitarian Association their terms together spanning nearly half a century. And there were many others; the Eliot genealogy is a veritable *Who's Who* of American Unitarianism.

In 1975 I preached a sermon marking the 140th Anniversary of the St. Louis church, a sermon highlighting some of the accomplishments of Eliot's life. After that, I had a question. Why wasn't this man better known, especially in St. Louis, a city which remembers its history better than most? Long ago I had observed the seemingly arbitrary vicissitudes of history. Some men rise in history's estimation, or at least in memory; others fall. Thomas Starr King, I had heard, was one of the best known men in the country at the time of his death in 1864, a national hero. But few even recognize his name today.

With Eliot I discovered there was something more than coincidence involved. He took deliberate steps to obliterate his place in history; he asked to be forgotten. Late in life he wrote out a series of requests, frequently re-dated and reiterated, asking that no memorials to him be constructed, no eulogies given, no biographies written. Though I am not the first to ignore these instructions, I have not been unmindful of them, and alongside them on the bulletin board above where I have occasionally worked on these essays, I have placed an excerpt from a funeral oration delivered by Eliot in the earliest years of his ministry in St. Louis for General William H. Ashley, a Missouri Congressman of considerable significance, who has also faded from the popular memory:

> No one who has laboured faithfully in a public sphere, or who has contributed in any important degree, to promote the public welfare, should be permitted to go down to the grave unnoticed: for not only do we confer honour upon ourselves, when we honour merit, but we give thereby a noble encouragement to the living, to imitate the virtues and aspire after the excellences of the dead. Honour to whom honour is due. We may justly deem it a religious duty, to be forward to inscribe upon the monuments of the dead, the record of their usefulness and of our gratitude; and especially are we bound not to forget those who were the pioneers, by whose enterprise the rough places of the West have been made smooth, and our fair and beautiful inheritance prepared for our own occupancy.

The same thing could have been said of Eliot 50 years later. We have it from him that it is nothing less than our religious duty to remember and honor those who have contributed so significantly to what we have and are, to write the record of their usefulness and our gratitude. This I have attempted to do, however inadequately, in the work which follows.

I said I am not the first. Eliot's daughter-in-law, Charlotte C. Eliot (mother of T. S. Eliot), wrote a full biography which was published by Houghton Mifflin in 1904. The organization of that work, pronounced "admirable" by at least one reviewer, was to take each area of Eliot's work and devote a chapter or two to it. Thus there are chapters on "Ministry," "Washington University," the "Western Sanitary Commission," and so on. This is a logical arrangement, but it gives a false impression. After all, Eliot was not only engaged in each of these enterprises but engaged in many of them simultaneously.

About the time I had realized that a full-scale biography was simply beyond the limits of the time I could possibly give to this work, an invitation to deliver the Minns Lectures prompted a decision to both limit the scope of the work and at the same time provide the perspective which the earlier biography had not. The six essays which follow are based upon the six Minns Lectures which I delivered in St. Louis in the fall of 1983. All but the last (and to some extent the first) take as a focal point a single year in Eliot's life. Obviously, these years were not randomly chosen, but each is suggestive of the wide range of activity which engaged Eliot throughout his life. Enough background is provided, it is hoped, to give some perspective on the events discussed, but for the most part each chapter limits itself to a single year. Additional material has been added between chapters, as a reminder that only a small part of the story is here being told.

*   *   *

It would be impossible to list all those who have assisted in some way in the completion of this work. The First Unitarian Church of St. Louis, to which it is Dedicated, through the many members of the congregation who have been unfailingly supportive of my ministry and particularly of this endeavor — a few of whom, sadly, died in the year before its publication and to whom a special dedication is offered — has provided encouragement as well as motivation. The Minns Committee of Boston provided generously not only for the original lectures but assisted financially in this publication; the support and encouragement of the Committee members and especially of its Chairman, Dr. James Jackson, is deeply appreciated.

I was assisted by staff members of a large number of institutions where Eliot materials are found, and, without exception, all were unfailingly helpful and generous of their time and expertise. Besides the major repository of Eliot materials at Washington University, other sources were: The Missouri Historical Society, St. Louis; the State Historical Society at Columbia, Missouri; the Andover-Harvard Library, Cambridge, Massachusetts (where assistance by Alan Seaburg and early guidance from C. Conrad Wright, Professor in the Divinity School, are remembered with appreciation); the libraries of Starr King School for the Ministry, Berkeley, California and Meadville Theological School, Chicago, Illinois; the library at Southern Illinois University, Edwardsville; and the Archives of the Unitarian Universalist Association, Boston.

I am deeply grateful to Dr. William H. Danforth, Chancellor of Washington University for contributing the Foreword, and to William Deiss, Deputy Archivist at the Smithsonian Institution Archives in Washington, D.C. and former Archivist at Washington University, for his introductory essay as well as for encouragement and advice based on his own Eliot researches.

Finally my deepest appreciation to Beryl Manne, Washington University Archivist, without whose cooperation and support this work would not have been begun, and to Marilyn G. Carpenter, Administrator of First Unitarian Church, without whose friendship and assistance it would never have been finished.

Earl K. Holt III
New York City
August 22, 1984

TABLE OF CONTENTS

ILLUSTRATIONS

CHRONOLOGY

1811 August 5 - William Greenleaf Eliot, Jr. (WGE) born at New Bedford, Massachusetts

1830 Graduates from Columbian College, Washington, D.C.

1834 Graduates from Harvard Divinity School, Cambridge, Massachuetts

1834 August 17 - Ordained as an Evangelist at Federal Street Church, Boston

1834 November 27 - Arrives in St. Louis

1835 January 26 - First Congregational Society of St. Louis formally organized

1837 June 29 - Marries Abby Adams Cranch (b. Febrary 20, 1817) in Washington, D.C.

1837 October 29 - Dedication of first church building, Northwest corner of 4th and Pine

1838 May 11 - Birth of Mary Rhodes Eliot, first of the 14 children born to the Eliots, 9 of whom died in infancy or youth

1847 February-October - First trip to Europe. In May WGE was elected General Secretary of the American Unitarian Association

1850-51 December-October - To Washington D.C. and second trip to Europe

1851 December 7 - Dedication of second church building, the Church of the Messiah, Northwest corner of 9th and Olive

1852 May 7-11 - Western Unitarian Conference organized, WGE elected its President

1853 February 22 - Wayman Crow's Charter for an "Eliot Seminary" (later Washington University) passed in the Missouri Legislature

1854 February 22 - First meeting of the Incorporators of Eliot Seminary, WGE elected President

1855 January 6 - Death of Mary Rhodes Eliot

1855 Publication of **The Discipline of Sorrow**

1855 Awarded the degree of Doctor of Divinity at Harvard

1857 April 22 - Formal Inaugural Exercises of Washington University at Mercantile Library Hall, lecture by Edward Everett

1857 May 24 - WGE preached "Social Reform" explaining the reasons for his withdrawal from the Western Unitarian Conference earlier in the month

1859 October 4 - Joseph G. Hoyt inaugurated as first Chancellor of Washington University

1861 August 18 - Preached "Loyalty and Religion"

1861 September 10 - Special Order No. 159, creating the Western Sanitary Commission

1862 February 5 - Rose Greenleaf Eliot (Smith) born, last of the Eliots' 14 children

1862 November 26 - Death of Chancellor Hoyt

1863 June 17 - Inauguration of William Chauvenet as Second Chancellor of Washington University

1869-70 September-April - Third trip to Europe

1870 May 15 - Dedication of the Church of the Unity, Park and Armstrong, Lafayette Square

1870 September 20 - Appointed Acting Chancellor of Washington University due to the serious illness of Chancellor Chauvenet, who died in December

1870 October 18 - Preached "Christ and Liberty," Conference Sermon for the Fourth Meeting of the National Unitarian Conference, New York City

1872 February 29 - Inauguration as Chancellor of Washington University

1873 April 20 - Installation of John Snyder as Minister of the Church of the Messiah

1881 December 16 - Dedication of the new Church of the Messiah, Northwest corner of Locust and Garrison

1885 Publication of **The Life of Archer Alexander**

1887 January 23 - The Rev. William Greenleaf Eliot, D.D. dies, at Pass Christian, Mississippi

INTRODUCTORY ESSAY

WILLIAM GREENLEAF ELIOT:
THE FORMATIVE YEARS (1811–1834)

by

William A. Deiss, Deputy Archivist

Smithsonian Institution Archives

Washington, D.C.

William G. Eliot, Jr. was born August 5, 1811, in New Bedford, Massachusetts, the third of eight children of William Greenleaf Eliot and Margaret Dawes Eliot. William G. Eliot, Sr. and his family moved to Baltimore soon after William's birth and, in 1818, to Washington, D.C., where the elder Eliot obtained a position as chief examiner in the Postal Department, a post which he retained until his retirement in 1853. From both parents young William inherited a distinguished and prominent ancestry. The Eliot family could trace its American lineage back to Andrew Eliot of East Coker, Somersetshire, who migrated to the colonies sometime between 1668 and 1670, and settled in Beverly, Massachusetts. In East Coker he had been a man of property and influence and a member of the Church of England; and he became a prominent citizen of Beverly, serving at various times as a member of the General Court, town clerk of Beverly, and a juror in the Salem Witch Trials.

His great grandson, the Rev. Andrew Eliot (1718–1778), became the first member of the family to graduate from Harvard. The son of a shoemaker and merchant of Boston, he received the degree of Bachelor of Arts in 1737 and the Master of Arts in 1740. The Rev. Andrew Eliot was one of the most distinguished American clergymen of the eighteenth century, serving as minister of the New North Church in Boston from 1742 to 1778. In 1767 he received the degree of Doctor of Sacred Theology from the University of Edinburgh, and served as a fellow of Harvard College from 1765 until his death in 1778. In 1773 he was elected to the presidency of Harvard, but refused the office because he was unwilling to leave his congregation.

Rev. Eliot's son, Samuel, was a merchant, Congregationalist, and Federalist of Boston who married into the Greenleaf family. His son, William Greenleaf Eliot, born in 1781, married his first cousin, Margaret Dawes of Boston in 1807 and moved to New Bedford. Margaret was the daughter of Judge Thomas Dawes and Margaret Greenleaf Dawes. Thomas Dawes was a member of a family that first appeared in Massachusetts in the mid-seventeenth century. From 1792 he served as a member of the Massachusetts Supreme Court, and from 1802 to 1825 as a Judge of Probate. His father, Colonel Thomas Dawes, a mason by trade, had been prominent in the political life of Massachusetts, and had been architect of the Brattle Street Church, supervising architect of the Massachusetts State House, and a vocal patriot during the Revolution.

The Greenleaf family also figured conspicuously in the ancestry of William G. Eliot, Jr. Both of his grandmothers were Greenleafs, the daughters of Sheriff William Greenleaf; and a third daughter, Nancy, married Judge William Cranch, and was to become Eliot's mother-in-law. The Greenleafs are thought to have been a Huguenot family which fled from France to England in the sixteenth century, from whence Edmund Greenleaf emigrated to America in 1635. A silk-dyer by trade, he kept a tavern in Newbury, Massachusetts, until he moved to Boston about 1650. His son, Stephen, was prominent in public affairs in Newbury, which he served as Representative to the General Court from 1676 to 1686. Stephen's son, Captain Stephen Greenleaf, was known as a great Indian fighter, and was also prominent in the political life of Massachusetts. The most prominent member of the family, however, was Sheriff William Greenleaf, born in 1725, the thirteenth and last child of Daniel Greenleaf. William Greenleaf was a merchant, but became active in the events of the Revolution. On November 2, 1772, he was one of seven chosen by the Boston Town Meeting to serve as a committee of correspondence with the other colonies in regard to measures to be pursued against the British. In 1775 he was appointed Sheriff of Suffolk, and in July 1776 he fulfilled his duty by reading the Declaration of Independence from the balcony of the Old State House. During the Revolution he financed privateers and reaped a profit of over £5,000.

William G. Eliot, Jr's. ancestors had been merchants, craftsmen, ministers, and public servants. Few, if any, had been wealthy, but neither had they been poor. All had their roots deep in the soil of New England. The Greenleafs, the Daweses, and the Eliots had been in New England for nearly two centuries before William's birth. They had been active and prominent in the affairs of both church and state. All were Congregationalists, men who believed in and practiced the New England virtues of sobriety and order.

William G. Eliot, Sr. was a merchant and shipowner in New Bedford when William Jr. was born in 1811. New Bedford was a prosperous whaling and shipping port of about three thousand people. The Revolutionary War had disrupted the economy of the town, but by about 1800 it had entered a period of growing prosperity. William Eliot had hoped to be a part of the prosperity when he settled there in 1807, but the embargo and the War of 1812 caused almost a complete suspension of trade out of New Bedford. Eliot suffered heavy losses, and as a result, moved his family to Baltimore, and in 1818, from there to Washington, D.C., where he received a position in the Postal Department, presumably through the good offices of his brother-in-law, William Cranch, who was Chief Justice of the United States Circuit Court in Washington.

In 1821 William Eliot, Sr. was one of the organizers of the First Unitarian Church in Washington. He was one of a small group of Unitarians who had begun meeting in 1820 in a room above a public bath to listen to the preaching of Robert Little, an Englishman who had been raised as a member of the Church of England, but had converted to Unitarianism and emigrated to the United States. Little was not an ordained minister, but he numbered among his congregation John Quincy Adams; John C. Calhoun; Charles Bullfinch, the architect; and Joseph Gales, who had been editor of the *Sheffield Register,* but had come to the United States because of his liberal political and religious ideas. Gales' son, Joseph Jr., was also a member, as was the latter's partner and editor of the *National Intelligencer,* William Winston Seaton, who also served several terms as Mayor of Washington. These men, together with Eliot and his brother-in-law, Judge William Cranch, were among the original members of the First Unitarian Church of Washington in 1821. The church was one of the first in the United States to openly avow its Unitarianism, the tendency having been to maintain the Congregational identity, although it embraced every range of opinion from Old Calvinism to liberalism.

Little's pastorate in Washington lasted until his death in 1827, a period during which he established himself as one of the finest preachers in the city. In 1824 Lafayette went to hear Little preach, and several times he preached before the House of Representatives on such subjects as "Religious Liberty and Unitarianism Vindicated," and "The Duty of Public Usefulness." On another occasion he delivered from his pulpit at the First Unitarian Church "a grand sermon, depicting with prophetic force the evils of General Jackson's election."

No record exists of young William's early education, but it could hardly have been lacking in a family which kept such company. It is safe to assume that he was raised on a diet of liberal religion (as defined in the 1820s), social respectability, public service, Federalism, and of course, the ever-present classics. His father earned his living first as a merchant and later as a civil servant; his maternal grandfather had been a judge; and his uncle, William Cranch had been one of President John Adams' midnight appointees, although he was later promoted by Jefferson. Judge Cranch was also the nephew of John Adams and the cousin of John Quincy Adams. William Eliot, Jr. was close to the Cranches, and became a close friend of his cousin, Christopher P. Cranch, with whom he later attended Columbian College and Harvard Divinity School. William was later to marry Christopher's sister, Abby Adams Cranch.

As a teenager William was sent back to New Bedford to attend the Friends' Academy. The Academy had been started in 1812 by a group of Quakers for the purpose of educating their children in the languages and liberal arts and sciences, while also ministering to their spiritual and moral needs. Children of Friends were to be given preference in admission, and the teachers were to be Quakers. But by the time of Eliot's attendance in the 1820s the original restrictions were no longer being enforced. The Academy was closed for one term in 1817, and in 1820, and did not officially reopen until 1827. But from 1824 to 1826 classes were taught in the school by George Newell, an 1823 graduate of Harvard. It is probable that Eliot attended the Academy during the years of Newell's supervision.

The years of Eliot's absence from New Bedford had been years of great turmoil in the religious life of the town. Between about 1810 and 1824 both the Congregational Church and the Society of Friends in New Bedford had split, with the liberal elements of each finally joining together in 1823 or 1824 as the First Congregational Society of New Bedford under the ministry of Orville Dewey, who arrived in the town in 1823 after two years as William Ellery Channing's assistant at the Federal Street Church in Boston.

In 1810 there had been a split within the Congregational ranks in New Bedford. A majority of the church members, who constituted a small minority of the parish, withdrew from the Society because of objections against the liberal tendencies of the majority of the parish, and of the proposed candidate for minister. They established the North Congregational Society in that year, which eventually split again into two divisions, while the original parish adopted a more liberal and generalized confession of faith and became progressively more Unitarian in the course of the next decade. The split within the Society of Friends was of the same nature, but in their case the liberals withdrew. The split occurred in 1823 when a revival began, spurred by "heretics" who had already caused a split within the Society of Friends in Lynn. The Old Lights (or conservatives) resented the emotionalism of the revivalists, and the ensuing struggle for the control of the New Bedford Meeting ousted the liberal members (New Lights).

Both splits were symptomatic of a general trend within the New England churches during that period. For about two decades after 1810 controversy raged in New England between conservatism and orthodoxy, on one hand, and liberal religion on the other. In essence, the splits within the ranks of both the Friends and the Congregationalists were over the same issues. In both instances the conservatives were extolling the virtues of doctrinal rigidity and biblical fundamentalism while the liberals were exalting the personal judgement and predilections of the individual at the expense of the traditional creeds, doctrines, and outward appurtenances of orthodoxy.

The most important men among the founders and initial trustees of the Friends' Academy were Samuel Rodman, William Rotch, and William Rotch, Jr. The Rotches and Rodmans were related by marriage, and formed two of the most important families in New Bedford. They were leaders of the New Light faction; and Mary Rotch, William's wife, later became a close friend of both Margaret Fuller and Ralph Waldo Emerson. The Rotches and Rodmans succeeded in 1823 in amending the charter of the Academy to state that a non-Quaker could serve as a member of the Board of Trustees if he had been a Quaker when elected, a move obviously in response to their expulsion from the New Bedford Meeting.

New Bedford, then, in 1824–1826 was a melting-pot in which two of the numerous strands of liberal religion were joined together in a common mixture. The extent of the influence of this stimulating religious atmosphere on William G. Eliot, Jr., can only be judged by conjecture. But in early nineteenth century New England, religion was the most prominent topic of thought and discussion among all classes.

The curriculum of the Friends' Academy in the years of Eliot's attendance there was probably the same as that listed in the catalog of 1830, the oldest that has been preserved. To be admitted to the Academy a student was expected only "to be able to read with facility common English authors, and his acquisitions in other respects such as may be thought necessary for attending the studies that he proposed to pursue." The Academy was primarily a college preparatory school with curriculum and textbooks, similar, if not identical, to those of the Boston Latin School. Pupils studied such subjects as Greek, Latin, and French, as well as English grammar and rhetoric, geography, natural philosophy, mathematics, moral philosophy, natural theology, and evidences of Christianity.

In 1826 William returned to Washington, where he entered Columbian College, a Baptist institution which had been founded in 1821 by the Rev. Luther Rice (1783–1836), a graduate of Andover Seminary. As a Congregational minister he had been instrumental in the founding of the American Board of Commissioners for Foreign Missions. However, while in Calcutta as a missionary he realized that he had become a Baptist in doctrine, and upon his return to the United States he affiliated with the Baptist Church.

Together with a group of associates Rice bought the land for the proposed college in the name of the Trustees of the Baptist Convention, and then sought a charter from Congress. But Congress refused to issue a charter for a denominational institution; and when the school finally received a charter in 1821 Congress stipulated that no denominational test would be permitted for either trustees, professors, tutors, or students. The land, however, was still owned by the Baptist Convention, most of the students were Baptists, and the Baptist denomination provided most of the financial support for the institution, and was able to maintain a good deal of control over the affairs of the institution. But that did not keep the Eliot and Cranch families from sending their children there. Thomas Dawes Eliot, William's older brother, was a member of the class of 1826, and at least three members of the Cranch family attended, as did two sons of Stephen Bullfinch.

The college course was divided into four departments: The Classical Department, the Theological Department, the Medical Department, and the Preparatory School. In 1826 a Law Department was instituted, and William Cranch was named one of the two professors, but the experiment was short-lived. Student records for the period do not exist, so we cannot be sure of what department Eliot studied in, but it seems doubtful that he would have chosen to study theology in a Baptist institution. It is also doubtful that at that time Eliot had yet decided on the ministry. A reasonable assumption would be that he studied in the Classical Department, the largest and most demanding of the school's departments.

After his graduation in 1830 William worked for a year as an assistant clerk in the chief examiner's room at the Postal Department in Washington, and in 1831 he enrolled in the Harvard Divinity School. Admissions standards at the Divinity School were stringent. Candidates, if unknown to the faculty, were required to "produce satisfactory testimonials of their moral and serious character . . . and to pass an examination in Hebrew Grammar and the first ten chapters of Deuteronomy." Candidates who were not graduates of "some respectable college" were also examined in

> . . . Latin and Greek Grammar, Virgil, Cicero's Select Orations, Sallust, Jacobs' Greek Reader, the extracts from Historians and Orators in the first volume of Collectanea Graeca Majora, Butler's Analogy, Locke's Essay, or some other treatise on Intellectual Philosophy, Paley's Moral Philosophy, or some other standard work on Ethics, and some approved compendium of Logic, Rhetoric, Geography, Arithmetic, Geometry, and Algebra.

The Divinity School had been established in 1811 at the instigation of the University's President, John Thornton Kirkland. Prior to that date theological instruction in preparation for the ministry had been largely informal. A prospective student usually took up residence in Cambridge or New Haven and attached himself to one of the Professors, from whom he received informal training in theology and ministerial duties. The alternative course was for parish ministers to take students into their homes and train them. This informal instruction, together with the occasional supplying of local pulpits, constituted the training of ministers in New England until divinity schools began to proliferate after 1808.

In that year the conservative Congregationalists founded Andover Theological Seminary in response to the Unitarian takeover of Harvard. In 1805, after extended debate, Henry Ware had been elected to the Hollis Professorship of Divinity; and in 1806 Samuel Webber was elected to the Presidency of Harvard. Unitarians now controlled the most prestigious chair in the University and the Presidency of the institution. In reaction to the apparent Unitarian takeover, the conservatives, led by Jedidiah Morse, Eliphalet Pearson, and Leonard Woods founded Andover as a bastion of consistent Calvinism.

Prior to 1805 New England Calvinism had been disintegrating from within. Three groups had formed: the liberals who had, in effect, rejected the major theological and philosophical tenets of Calvinism; the consistent Calvinists who adhered strictly to the orthodox doctrines of total depravity and predestination; and a large group of moderates who claimed to be strict Calvinists, but who had softened the harsher tenets of Calvinism through metaphysical inconsistencies that presented man with a somewhat more benign God and a better hope for salvation.

The events of 1805–1806 and the resulting controversy served to accentuate the tensions within the Standing Order and led to a polarization of opinion. The moderates, fearing heresy and infidelity, fled to the camp of the Hopkinsians (or conservatives), and, in 1808, established the theological school at Andover as a means of nipping the insurrection in the bud by providing a constant supply of conservative ministers. The liberals, few of whom would have dared call themselves Unitarians, were a fragmented group, loosely allied at best. The founding of Andover, however, forced them into each other's arms, and led in 1811 to the beginnings of systematic instruction in divinity at Harvard.

The three decades following the election of Ware to the Hollis Professorship were decades of controversy between the liberal and conservative wings of Congregationalism. During this period the liberal wing decisively eschewed Calvinism and became a denomination. As the Unitarians defined their position various doctrinal differences with the Calvinists became obvious, such as the former's adherence to Arminianism and the doctrine of the Unity of God as opposed to the concept of the Trinity. But the major difference was in their view of the nature of man. The Unitarians saw man as the image of God, putting more trust in intuition and man's ability to reason and to interpret the Scriptures, while the Calvinists adhered to a belief in man's depraved nature and his dependence upon the absolute literal truth of the Bible.

By 1831, when Eliot entered the Divinity School, Unitarianism had established itself on firm ground in the area of Boston, while the rural areas of New England remained Calvinist. As a result of the pamphlet warfare conducted by Henry Ware of Harvard and Leonard Woods of Andover, the Unitarian position had been relatively well defined, even though there were many disputed points within the ranks of the liberals. It was as a mild and refined faith, rather than as a body of doctrine, that Unitarianism emerged during this period. It was at the ordination of the Rev. Jared Sparks in Baltimore in 1819 that Unitarianism received its classical definition and emerged as a dynamic faith. In his sermon on "Unitarian Christianity" delivered at Sparks' ordination William Ellery Channing finally pulled together the ravelled threads of liberalism into a statement of faith that, at least to a certain extent, united the ranks of the liberals and established him as the spiritual leader of the movement in America.

Channing exalted reason, individuality, and progress in opposition to orthodoxy and systems of authority which were repugnant not only to the precepts of Christianity, but to the nature of man. He extolled the use of reason in interpreting the Scriptures, and the value of Biblical and historical scholarship in helping man understand the Scriptures. Contradictions and unreasonable passages in the Bible, he contended, must be subjected to philological and historical analysis in order to separate myth or the additions of fallible men from the fundamental principles of Christianity put forth by revelations. He attempted not only to establish the positive beliefs of Unitarians, but to destroy the irrational and confining effects of orthodoxy and Biblical fundamentalism.

He discussed the major positions of Unitarian belief and attempted to explain that they were the result of trying to divine the general principles of Christianity and rid it of its contradictions and man-made impurities. He denied the doctrine of the Trinity in favor of the Unity of God as well as the Unity of Jesus Christ. The doctrine of the Trinity was not taught in the Bible nor was it taught by the apostles; it was an invention of latter-day theologians. God is the Father and Christ is a distinct and inferior being by his own admission. He rejected the Calvinist doctrines of predestination and innate depravity as ridiculous and contrary to the nature of God, whom he saw as both just and merciful. Calvinism could not reconcile God's justice with mercy; it made God into a cruel and willful tyrant devoid of love and incapable of being loved or respected. Christ's mission was not to serve as the object of God's wrath, but to serve as an example to mankind.

Channing viewed man as essentially a moral creature capable of achieving salvation. Christian virtue lay not in election, but in love of God and in the effort to achieve moral perfection and lead a Christian life. He saw neither excitement nor outward show, but character, as the essence of religion. He felt that the goals of the Reformation had been obscured by a new authoritarianism. Men had overthrown the dominance of the papacy only to create in its place a type of Papal Protestantism. Channing contended that Unitarianism was carrying on the principle of the Reformation in an attempt to sweep away the human inventions that were imposing a new intolerance. The goal of Unitarianism was to overturn old hierarchies and man-made institutions that served only to retard the development of the individual and the progress of society.

The two major characteristics of Unitarianism, as defined by Channing, were the exaltation of the individual and the deprecation of outward enthusiasm in religion. The first of these was founded upon a reinterpretation of the nature of God, and consequently, of his creature, man. Man was no longer viewed as sinful and degraded, but as a creature made in God's image with the reasoning power necessary to understand the word of God, and with the moral capability to ensure unlimited progress. The deprecation of enthusiasm in favor of character development and piety reflected a new image of the Christian man. Aside from doctrinal differences these were the major presuppositions upon which Unitarians based their rejection of the old Calvinism. But, they had in them the germs that were to lead, in the 1830s and 1840s, to the Transcendental revolt within the ranks of the Unitarians.

The importance of Channing's sermon lies not in the fact that it was the first statement of Unitarian belief, nor that it was the only statement, nor even that it spoke for all Unitarians, but that it was the best summary yet to emerge of a faith which, admittedly, in 1819, was floundering for lack of definition and cohesiveness. Unitarianism was never to achieve any sort of real uniformity or cohesiveness, but it was to achieve a community of sorts (albeit defensive in nature) and a general set of principles and beliefs. It was never able to agree to a creed, but it had at least been defined in general terms.

Arminianism had been developing within the ranks of Congregationalism for many years prior to the open break that occurred after 1805. At that point the Unitarians were the liberals fighting against the conservatism of the Standing Order. The period of the Unitarian controversy and the denominational consolidation of Unitarianism is usually dated from 1805 to 1838, in which year Ralph Waldo Emerson delivered his famous Divinity School Address. According to the traditional account, the two decades after 1838 were the period in which Unitarianism fought with a strangely conservative zeal against the heresy implicit in the transcendental philosophy. In reality, the beginnings of Transcendentialism can be traced back to the 1820s when, at Harvard, the ministerial students were doing a bit more than listening to Henry Ware and reading their Paley.

The emphasis upon individual capability was simply carried to its logical extension in the mysticism and rampant individualism of the Transcendentialists. Certainly they read the English romantics and the German philosophers, but they were receptive to their message because of their Unitarian background. It was not by chance that Emerson delivered his famous address before the graduates at Harvard instead of those at Andover or Yale. On the other hand, the essentially quiet, undemonstrative nature of Unitarian belief with its emphasis upon character and the Christian life as opposed to revivalism and stirring sermons, led to a coldness and conservatism that was, in effect, repudiated by the Transcendentalists. Boston Unitarianism was the domain of the rich and the self-satisfied. It lost its dynamism (if it ever had any) and became "corpse-cold." The younger generation of aspiring preachers who reached their maturity after about 1830 were not only bored by the deadness of their churches, but were in revolt against them.

It was in this context, in the beginning of the turmoil, that William Greenleaf Eliot, Jr. journeyed to Cambridge in 1831 to study for the ministry. At Harvard the two contending forces that were soon to rend the fabric of Unitarianism were in evidence. The faculty represented the old guard. They were not reactionaries, but they were men of an earlier era. By the Calvinists, they were considered liberals, but by many of their students they were viewed as men mired in the formalism and rationalism of the eighteenth century.

There were three major professors at the Divinity School during Eliot's period of attendance: Henry Ware, Henry Ware, Jr., and John Gorham Palfrey. The elder

Ware had been Hollis Professor of Divinity since his controversal appointment to the chair in 1805. Ware, who was sixty-seven years of age in 1831, was largely self-educated, with little formal schooling as a boy. But by 1781, at the age of fifteen he had prepared himself well enough to be admitted to Harvard.

After his graduation in 1785 he taught school in Cambridge for a year; and in 1787 he became pastor of the parish church in Hingham, a position he retained until his election to the Hollis Professorship in 1805. The controversy that began as a result of his election reached its peak when, in response to criticism by Leonard Woods, he replied and initiated a controversy that became known as the Wood 'n' Ware debate. In 1811 he began a course of exercises with resident students in divinity that was the germ of the Divinity School.

Ware's religious thought had been formulated by the time of his appointment to the Hollis Professorship in 1805 and remained unchanged throughout his tenure of thirty-five years. He instructed his students in natural religion and the evidences of revealed religion, a subject on which, by 1812, he had completed 168 lectures which he delivered one a week in a four-year cycle, repeated again and again for thirty-five years, and finally published in 1840 under the title *An Inquiry into the Foundation Evidences, and Truths of Revealed Religion.*

He conducted classes on the same topic with all three classes in the Divinity School. The exercises were held weekly and lasted for two to three hours each. Each week he assigned a topic on which the students were to write an essay. In each instance he recommended authorities to be consulted, most of whom were eighteenth century English divines. When the class met next week he selected a student who would read his entire essay; the remainder of the students in order were required to read what they had written that differed from the first. In the discussions that followed, Ware was known for his disinterestedness and impartiality.

Ware was, by no means, an original scholar. He was a representative of the Arminian phase of the Unitarian movement, and it must have been obvious to his students. He gave them little more than had been given him half a century earlier. He was as out of tune with the rigorous Biblical criticism of his colleagues Andrews Norton and John Gorham Palfrey as he was with the newly emerging German criticism, which he could not read had he so desired, because of his ignorance of the language. He was an eighteenth century rationalist unaware of the new currents of thought coming to the fore in the 1830s. His colleagues loved and respected him, as did his students, but it is little wonder that the latter began to turn elsewhere for nourishment.

Henry Ware, Jr. was not as concerned with theology and doctrine as were his father and his colleague, John Gorham Palfrey. He was conservative in his theology, but it took second place in his mind to his duties as a minister. He was interested in the practical duties of the pastoral office and the character and role of the minister. He was recognized as the greatest minister of his day, and he imparted his concept of that office to his students. In this role, combined with his great personal warmth and constant contact with, and interest in, his students, he was probably the greatest personal influence in the life of William Eliot. Ware's concept of the ministry was reflected in Eliot's career, and although, while at Cambridge, Eliot, in his youthful enthusiasm and forays into metaphysics, occasionally complained of the overly practical nature of the instruction at the Divinity School, he absorbed all that he could from Ware.

Henry Ware, Jr. had inherited his father's theological conservatism, but while the elder Ware was found by his students to be ". . . too logical, sensible, moderate, and unimaginative . . . ," his son was a teacher of rare ability. His rapport with his students was remarkable. His home was always open to them and he was a welcome and frequent visitor to their lodgings. He was a virtual invalid, having resigned as pastor of the Second Church in Boston because of ill health to accept what he felt would be less rigorous duties as a professor in the Divinity School. He accepted the Professorship of Pulpit Eloquence and Pastoral Care in 1823, but because of his health did not enter upon his duties until 1830. Yet the day was not long enough for what he felt to be his duties to his students. He catered to their needs as individuals and had a great sense of the individual differences and capacities of his students, carefully gained from close and constant intercourse with them.

The subjects that he taught were the art of composition, composition of sermons, prayer and public devotion, pastoral duty, elocution, and extemporaneous speaking. He seldom lectured, although he occasionally delivered courses of lectures on selected topics; and at the beginning of each term he delivered a lecture to the entire student body "on some topic of personal and professional character, e.g. *Importance of Piety in a Minister, The Spirit of the Profession, Clerical Prudence,* etc." He preferred discussion with his students, for which they met in class twice a week to discuss the art of writing sermons or pastoral duty. The students prepared sermons which were then discussed and criticized by Ware in a manner designed to encourage rather than discourage them.

On Friday evening the senior and middle classes preached extempore in rotation, and received Ware's criticisms. On Saturday evenings the same students preached before the entire faculty. Ware then took the sermons home and invited one of the preachers to his home for breakfast on a specified morning shortly afterward. After breakfast and family worship the student and teacher would retire to Ware's study for a long and detailed discussion and dissection of the sermon.

Ware was interested in both the practical aspects of the ministerial profession and the role of the minister as a man of God and a teacher of morals. In a series of lectures on pastoral care he dealt with such specifics as the intricacies of establishing, administering, and teaching Sunday School; instruction of young men and women and of families; pastoral visits to the sick and the afflicted; and the proper time for, and conduct of, baptism, marriage, communion, and funerals. In the final lecture of the series he presented the young men with a "Plan for a Successful Ministry," in which he recommended cultivation of the religious character and devotion to the profession and to study. He recommended that the minister divide his time systematically between "Study" and "Active Engagement."

Ware constantly tried to impress upon his charges that the key to a successful ministry was the complete integration of the duties of the preacher and the pastor. Each depended on the other, and neither, in itself, could lead to success. In fact, Ware chose "The Connexion Between the Duties of the Pulpit and the Pastoral Office" as the topic of his introductory address before the members of the Divinity School in 1830. He contended that

> The connexion . . . between the eloquence of the Pulpit and the Pastoral Care is real and natural. These two branches go together and sustain each other. The minister is a better preacher for having his heart warmed by intercourse with his hearers in private; and he goes to them in private with the greater influence and effect, because he carried with him the sacredness and sanction of the Pulpit. The full power of the Christian Ministry can be known only where both departments are exercised with faithfulness; and he entirely errs, who fancies that he may neglect either and yet command the best success in the other. It is to the union of the two that we must look for the efficient and complete minister.

He felt that the object of the ministry was the reformation of individuals and the formation of a Christian character, and ultimately, through the improvement of individuals, the general improvement of society. Ware argued, as Eliot was to do later, that too many ministers saw Christianity as a vehicle for the direct improvement of society; Christianity must act upon individuals, and ultimately, but only indirectly, on society. He felt that too many ministers preached to, and treated, the members of the congregation as a congregation, not as individuals. The minister's pastoral duties would serve to help him get to know his parishioners and to understand their faults as well as their strengths. This personal knowledge would supply the preacher with the raw material for meaningful sermons; while, on the other hand, his duties as a preacher would enhance his authority and position, and thus make him more effective in the implementation of his pastoral duties, and in his ultimate goal of reformation and perfection of the individual under his charge.

The complete integration of the minister's duties, and the necessity of single-minded devotion to them, was the gospel that Henry Ware, Jr. preached to his students; and William G. Eliot listened intently. Of all the voices that William heard in his years at Harvard, Ware's was the loudest and most influential. Eliot studied theology and Biblical criticism under the elder Ware and John Gorham Palfrey, and he dabbled in German metaphysics and Transcendentalism under the tutoring of James Freeman Clarke and William Henry Channing; but the duties and cares of the ministry were to be the most important considerations in his life. Eliot was by nature a doer, and Henry Ware, Jr. told him what to do and how to do it.

John Gorham Palfrey became the third member of the Divinity School triumvirate in 1831 when he was appointed Dean of the Divinity School and Dexter Professor of Biblical Literature. As a student he had entered Harvard in 1811 at the age of fifteen, where he studied Greek under Edward Everett, Hebrew under Sidney Willard, and Biblical criticism under Buckminster, Channing, and Norton. He was a rationalist, a logician, a student of Locke and Paley, Levi Hedge, and Dugald Stewart. As Dean of the Divinity School he reorganized the curriculum, deemphasizing the elder Ware's courses in natural and revealed religion and ecclesiastical history, and establishing four main areas of study: criticism of the New Testament, criticism of the Old Testament, the composition of sermons, and Hebrew and German.

Andrews Norton, Palfrey's predecessor, and Professor of Sacred Literature had been known for his great scholarship, but also for his dogmatism and arrogant assurance of the correctness of his opinions. Palfrey

> on the other hand, with hardly less fixedness of opinion, admitted his own fallibility, invited discussion, welcomed the expression of non-agreement, and even asked his students to prepare in writing, and read to the class, their reasons for differing from him.

Palfrey taught Hebrew and the exegesis of the New Testament, the latter of which was his major field of interest, and upon which he published two works based upon his lectures at the Divinity School: *Academical Lectures on the Jewish Scriptures and Antiquities* in four volumes (1838–1852) and *The Relation Between Judaism and Christianity* (1854). In addition, he regularly gave instruction in Syriac, Arabic, and Biblical Aramaic in successive years in rotation. He was dissatisfied with the texts available, so he mastered all the Semitic languages and wrote his own textbooks in 1835, thus allowing his students to read the entire Old Testament in Chaldean.

In addition to his course work, Palfrey delivered many sermons in the college chapel; and a description of his style penned by one of his students is worthy of extensive quotation:

> Dr. Palfrey's style of composition for the pulpit was unique, and I have always ascribed its peculiarities to his minute and painstaking truthfulness. Afraid of overstatement, he inserted in a single sentence all needed qualifications, exceptions, and explanations, so that the sentence might stand by itself in representing

precisely what he meant to convey neither more nor less. His sentences were, therefore, packed so full of meaning as to seem to the eye involved and obscure. But not so to the ear. He had what I might call a pictorial mode of utterance, a vocal *chiaro-scuro,-* so that it was easy to give its due light or shadow to each general statement, to every modifying clause, and to parenthesis within parenthesis, even to the third degree. His delivery was animated without being impassioned; and to the hearer perspicuity equally with precision, characterized his discourse.

The nature of Palfrey's preaching was in many ways illustrative of the nature of instruction at the Harvard Divinity School. The teaching was judicious and restrained as was Boston Unitarianism in general. Emphasis was upon biblical criticism and scholarship rather than dogmatic theology. As Conrad Wright has pointed out, at Andover one of the five professorships was in Christian theology; but at Harvard such a thing was unthinkable. The students were given the tools of Biblical criticism so that they might be able to pursue truth as individuals. Dogma was anathema; uniformity of opinion was neither enforced nor expected. Enthusiasm was discouraged in favor of rationality and character formation. The goal was not indoctrination, but guidance and instruction. The students were expected to think for themselves; and, as a result of the emphasis upon self-culture and of the somewhat cold and overly-rational nature of Unitarianism, a good number of them began a quiet revolt, that was in essence, an exaltation of the individual mind and a rejection of the Lockean and Scottish systems of philosophy that underlay much of Unitarian thought.

Student life at the Divinity School revolved not only around the formal course of instruction. Students did not spend more than a few hours a day in class, and the rest of the day was free for individual study. The students boarded on campus in Divinity Hall and thus became quite close. Eliot, soon after his arrival, became acquainted with two of his fellow students, James Freeman Clarke and William Henry Channing, both of whom were a year ahead of him. The three of them became close friends; and it was Clarke who later arranged for Eliot to go to St. Louis. Many years later, in a eulogy to Eliot, Clarke mentioned that he and Eliot and William Henry Channing saw each other every day,

and our conversation was on the most important themes, William Eliot was more practical, William Channing more ideal. Like all sincere souls, each of these men valued in the other that in which the other excelled himself.

Just prior to Eliot's arrival at the Divinity School in 1831, a group of students, at the suggestion of Henry Ware, Jr., had formed a Philanthropic Society. Several members of the school had been teaching Sunday School at the state prison at Charlestown, and had attempted to find employment for released convicts. The Society was formed to aid in the enterprise, in addition to serving as a debating society. The subjects debated were the major social issues and reforms of the day. Most, if not all of the students, belonged to the Society, and Eliot, together with Channing and Clarke, was among the original members in 1831.

William entered heartily into the work of the Philanthropic Society. Meetings were held about every two weeks, and the debates were exercises in the rhetoric and methods of moral reform. Among the subjects discussed were the colonization of free blacks, foreign missions, intemperance, western missionary work, prison reform, infidelity, the state of education in manufactories, Bible societies, Sunday School, reform of the drama, pauperism, the treatment of the insane, Universalism, and the means for increasing the supply of ministers. The goals were essentially conservative in nature, and reflected the state of Unitarian social thought. Unitarians were liberal Christians, but were essentially conservative of the established institutions of society. The emphasis in the debates was not on social reform, but on moral reform.

At each regular meeting, the Society selected a subject, which was referred to a committee of three students, who were to submit a report on it at the next meeting, where it was debated and discussed. Eliot's activities as a member of the Society were concentrated primarily on the study of the western missionary movement and the study of prison discipline. On September 19, 1832, he read a report on Bible societies before the Society; and in June 1833 he joined in a discussion of the state of popular education in America. In November of that year he joined in discussing the subject of pauperism, as a result of which discussion it was resolved that "all permanent provision for the poor, except in particular cases, hospitals, workhouses, houses of correction, and almshouses, is injudicious." At the same meeting he proposed as a subject for a report "whether any and what systematic means should be taken to spread Liberal Christianity through the country," a subject on which he reported to Society the following January. Eliot's connection with the Philanthropic Society, however, was mostly through his interest in prison discipline. The Society was originally formed to implement the students' attempts at preaching to and reforming convicts; and Eliot entered into that activity with a vigor and interest that continued throughout his life. In October 1832, he was appointed, together with William Henry Channing, a member of the five-man standing committee on prisons; and in that capacity he read a report on prisons to the Society in September 1833, to which he attached the following resolution: "Resolved: That the States-Prison at Charlestown and the Jail at Lockmere Point afford fields of useful exertion, in which it is our duty to labor according to our ability, and that increased activity in both of them is exceedingly desirable." It was voted to accept Eliot's report, the text of which no longer exists; but the discussion of the resolution was postponed indefinitely, and it apparently never was accepted.

Eliot, however, continued to spend a good deal of his time implementing his rejected resolution. His spare time was spent in visiting the poor, and examining jails, asylums, and hospitals. He taught Sunday School at various times at Charlestown State Prison, the Boston Leverett Street Jail, and the jail at Lockmere Point. Many years later, in an address delivered before the National Prison Discipline Association, Eliot described his experiences:

> I cannot help smiling now, when I think of my utter unfitness for the work. A very young man, not yet fairly out of boyhood, as thoroughly inexperienced in the world's ways as a little girl, as verdantly green with respect to the dark iniquities of criminal life as it was conveniently possible to be; brought there into immediate contact with the rugged and hardened outcasts of society, who had sounded the depths and explored the obscure places of the deadliest sin, they must have looked upon me with half amusement and half surprise . . . To confess the truth, I fear I taught them very little, and perhaps did them but little good. But, what is more to the purpose, they taught me a great deal, and I am inclined to think that not even . . . the best of my theological instructors, although the sainted Henry Ware was among them, conferred upon me greater benefit, or more lasting good, than I received, unwittingly, from these Pariahs of the human race. For they taught me that the prison holds human hearts, and that those whom we call vile, and upon whom the scourge of justice most heavily and most justly falls, are as open to the influence of sympathy and as grateful for the word of kindness, and as ready to meet, half way, every sincere effort for their reform, and as deserving of friendly regard, as many of those who say, "God . . . I thank thee that I am not as other men are."

Not all of William's time, however, was devoted to the implementation of "practical Christianity." His spare time was spent in the company of his two closest friends among his classmates, James Freeman Clarke and William Henry Channing. His relationship with Clarke was very close and was in essence that of teacher and pupil, with Eliot the dutiful pupil. Channing's relationship with Eliot was evidently warm but each was closer to Clarke than to the other. Eliot was practical and conservative, and perhaps a bit unintellectual, while Channing was mystical and preeminently impractical. Clarke seemed to bridge the gap between them and bring them closer than their divergent personalities would normally have allowed.

The Divinity School students, along with the other youthful citizens of Cambridge, formed two divergent social groupings. One group formed about Clarke's two cousins, Helen and Margaret Davis, while the other formed around the brilliant, but often distant, Margaret Fuller. The former group engaged in a round of parties, excursions and balls; the other was more literary in nature, and its members read Coleridge, Wordsworth, Lamb, Carlyle, and Sir Thomas Browne in addition to the German writers, Goethe, Schiller, Lessing, Tiech, Novalis, and Richter. The group really constituted the first school of Transcendentalism in America. Its members included, among others, Margaret Fuller, William Henry Channing, Henry Hedge, and Elizabeth Peabody, all of whom were later to be early members of the Hedge Club. While Clarke moved with facility between both groups, Eliot's position is unclear; apparently he was a member of neither group, but on the fringe of both because of his friendship with Clarke.

Clarke and Margaret Fuller had met in 1829, the year of his graduation from Harvard College, while Channing had known her casually since she had been a schoolmate of his sister's in Boston; and he and Clarke had been friends since their years together at the Boston Latin School and at Harvard College. The three were close friends and had travelled in the same social circles in Boston and Cambridge long before Eliot arrived in Cambridge in 1831.

While Eliot was concerning himself with the Philanthropic Society and visiting prisons and almshouses, Clarke, Channing and Margaret Fuller were delving into the metaphysical subtleties of German philosophy and poetry. Clarke was introduced to German philosophy and literature in 1829, when he read Carlyle's articles in the *Edinburgh Review* on "The State of German Literature," "Richter," and his "Essay on Goethe," and began reading Coleridge's *The Friend, Aids to Reflection, and Biographia Literaria* which had recently been reprinted by President James Marsh of Vermont University. During the same year he met Margaret Fuller, and a close friendship rapidly developed between them.

During his first year at the Divinity School Clarke had been very unhappy and discouraged. His discovery of Coleridge and Carlyle had led him to reject the materialism taught at Harvard, but as yet he had found nothing with which to replace it. He was floundering philosophically — searching for a system of thought, a meaning to life. Margaret Fuller filled the void; she was "a gift of the gods, an influence like no other." She seemed to have a purpose in life, a direction to her study. She was further advanced than Clarke, and she encouraged him and led him with her into a new world. Margaret was primarily a critic; she was very sure of herself and capable of making quick and brilliant judgements. To Clarke and the small group of Cambridge students who gathered about her, she was seen as a prophetess. She could be very warm and vital to those in whom she saw a kindred spirit, but very cold and distant to others. Together, in the spring of 1832, she and Clarke began to study German and mastered it within three months. During the next year Margaret read "Goethe's Faust, Tasso, Iphigenie, Hermann and Dorothea, Elective Affinities and Memoirs; Tieck's William Lovell, Prince Zerbino and other works; Korner and Novalis, and something of Richter; all of Schiller's principal dramas and his lyric poetry." Clarke, on the other hand, claimed to have read within the next two years, "thirty or forty volumes of Goethe — six or seven Schiller, some of Tieck, Richter, Novalis, Schleiermacher, Jacobi. . . ."

William Eliot was introduced to German philosophy by Clarke. Eliot questioned the worth of his friend's preoccupation with philosophy while the practical work of Christian teaching and benevolence was so urgent and pressing. But he began to feel the need to balance his external work with intellectual work, and at Clarke's recommendation he read Fichte's *Bestimmung des Menschen*. Soon after introducing Eliot to German literature Clarke was ordained, and accepted the call of a small Unitarian Society in Louisville. At the same time William Henry Channing also completed his studies, and although he remained in Cambridge, Eliot did not see as much of him as previously. During the 1833–1834 school year, Eliot was placed upon his own resources. He was trying to establish his identity, and prepare himself for the ministry. He missed his close friendship with Clarke and unburdened himself in the letters that he wrote to his friend in Louisville. He occasionally saw Margaret Fuller who was staying in Cambridge with the Farrars', but her attitude toward him bordered on patronizing contempt. In September 1833 William spent an evening in conversation with Margaret, at the Farrar's, and Margaret arranged for him to board with them. On his occasional meetings with her she was "as witty and intellectual as ever." He still occasionally saw William Channing and often visited Clarke's grandfather, James Freeman. He attended William Ellery Channing's Federal Street Church and apparently often went to the elder Channing for counsel and advice. During the year he was forced by financial difficulties to accept an instructorship in Hebrew at the College, and he often spent his evenings attending public lectures. In September William wrote to Clarke telling him of a lecture by Edward Everett on "Education" that had been essentially Lockean and that had denied the central tenets of Phrenology, "that there is an original and irremovable difference in minds." Eliot and Clarke in addition to a good many of their acquaintances were believers in Phrenology, but Everett's speech had caused him to reassess his position. "I was going a little too *blindly* with that doctrine. I believe it, indeed, but must not let that belief lead me to underestimate the immense, the incalculable power of education; which after all 'in the long run' makes the difference between men." As Eliot continued he began to show the effects of his reading in German:

I should have full faith in my power to direct my own mind, to make myself, under God, what I please to be; should I not? Is not such faith well grounded? I may not be able to become a poet, nor shall attempt it: yet who may set a limit to the attainments of *any* mind which is governed by a strong will, and is full of spiritual faith?

In the same month, Eliot preached his first sermon before the entire school on the subject of philanthropy, and received from Henry Ware, Jr., the rather strange comment that "it was a promising beginning for a youth of my age and advantages." Ware's comment reflected an attitude held by others, including Clarke and Fuller, that Eliot was not quite on an intellectual par with his fellow students. Margaret Fuller viewed Eliot with a mild contempt, and Clarke considered Eliot a "*disciple* of mine." Even though Eliot and Clarke were extremely close, their relationship was one in which Clarke predominated. Clarke's depiction of Eliot as his disciple hardly implied equality.

The answer probably lies both in William's academic preparation prior to his matriculation at Harvard, and his predilection toward the practical. Eliot was not a Harvard graduate, and until the mid-1830s it was rare for someone not a graduate of Harvard to attend the Divinity School. While Clarke and Channing and their classmates were reading the English romantics, Eliot was attending the Baptist-oriented Columbian College. The Transcendental movement began in Boston; the entire movement was a Boston phenomenon. Eliot was probably completely unaware of the beginnings of the movement when he reached Cambridge. To his fellow students he appeared naive, and there was probably an element of Boston snobbery involved in their feelings toward him. In addition, when he was introduced to German thought he probably did not grasp it as eagerly as some of his friends because of his conservative nature and interest in the practical work of the ministry.

From about 1832 or 1833 on, at any rate, Eliot dabbled in German philosophy and literature. It is difficult to determine where and when he learned to read German, but he did. He did not learn it at Columbian College for it was not part of the curriculum. In 1826 the Divinity School had hired a part-time instructor in German, and in 1821 it was recommended that German be required of first-year students in the Divinity School, but there is some doubt that it was required or even taught regularly. Clarke claimed that he learned German together with Margaret Fuller in the spring of 1832, yet he had entered the Divinity School in 1830, which indicates that he had received no instruction in the language at Harvard. Eliot, however, could read German well enough to begin his studies in it before Clarke left for Louisville, and continued them through at least 1834. Clarke was the teacher and Eliot the pupil in transcendental realms.

Transcendentalism was a protest against the coldness and conservatism of Boston Unitarianism. It was, as Perry Miller defined it, essentially "a religious demonstration . . . an expression of religious radicalism in revolt against a rational conservatism . . . a protest of the human spirit against emotional starvation."

Among the Harvard students it constituted a search for a deeper meaning for their lives, a revival couched in literary terms. Clarke found himself in German literature, but floundered in Louisville; Eliot floundered and thrashed on the surface of German literature, but found himself in St. Louis.

In October, Eliot wrote Clarke a long letter baring his doubts and yearnings to his friend. He had been working on a sermon on faith and in the process had undergone a period of self-doubt and examination. He was searching for truth, a reason for existence and felt that he had found it in laboring diligently in the service of God and in complete and unquestioning faith. He felt that he had no one to share his thoughts with since Clarke had left.

> I have now no intimate friend; none with whom I really *converse.* I know not how it is, but there seems to be want of individuality to the thoughts of all I talk with *now;* they may be good thoughts, but not the result of their own reflection, 'delving and diving for principles;' *collected* and perhaps collated; let me use a word which is more meaning [sic] to you than to me, there is little *German.* Our school is run mad with the *Practical.* Now the tendency of all my studies up to this time has been practical — but I have come to see that, as you say, 'speculating somewhat' is the true way to become practical. You cannot tell how much I feel the want of deep, abstract study; I feel drawn as if by a strong cord, to German; and am now reading Fichte (Sonnen Klanen &c). I do not know how it is, but I do not take the pleasure that I used to in reading English books — they never before seemed so much on the surface; while Principles are what my nature is craving . . . I have only practical good sense in answer to a speculation.

He feared that because of his lack of great truths and principles he would not be ready to preach within a year. In short, Eliot was going through the period of anxiety and self-doubt that Clarke endured a few years before, and had escaped from with the help of Margeret Fuller and German philosophy.

Eliot, however, still questioned the usefulness of German philosophy. He feared that too much study of transcendental notions might cause him to become "a dreaming, skeptical or mystical being, and forever be held back from progress by this one sad mistake." He felt that he must not delve into transcendental realms without first anchoring his soul to faith, by which he meant "real faith in the

16

existence of truth." He believed that there was only one philosophy and one religion, and one stream of truth which man must strive for because it was the essence of religious faith. The pursuit of truth as he understood it, led him down the path of duty. The belief in truth, he felt, enlarged his idea of duty and freed it from utilitarianism.

After receiving encouragement in his speculations from Clarke, and receiving a new list of German books to read, Eliot again wrote to Clarke. William had been reading Goethe's *Wilhelm Meister* and reported himself "very much enraptured with it . . . I tell you that I have not found one sentiment expressed for which there is not some response in myself." *Wilhelm Meister* was a spiritual biography which Clarke considered a guide to his own life, and he was very pleased with his "student" for his interpretation of Wilhelm. In a letter to Margaret Fuller, Clarke commented on Eliot's development:

> Eliot's letter rejoices me. It relieves my mind from the doubt which sometimes besets it, that the ideas I was grafting in would not suit well his previous practical and mechanical habits. I rejoice to find that these ideas are pervading and regenerating his whole intellectual and (by consequence) moral nature, and are giving a new and healthy life to his system which was withering in dissatisfaction for the want of such a stimulus and food.

On the same day as his letter to Margaret Fuller, Clarke replied to Eliot's letter of February 2 congratulating him on his attainment of intellectual maturity.

> I am much delighted with your way of thinking — I rejoice in your extraordinary improvement, mental and moral, during the past year — I congratulate you upon your complete emancipation from all contracted maxims and spiritless forms. Your last letter was written with such united freedom and strength that it assured me that you had passed with safety the critical period involved in every great change in the leading principles of our life. I used to have lurking dread when talking to you, that I might be injuring you by leading you into a transcendental region not suited to the senses, organs, and possessions with which your mind was already furnished. But that fear is over. The strong and disinterested love of Truth which animated you has carried you safely on, and now your new principles seem thoroughly to have pervaded your mind, and I recognize no longer any clashings between the practical and spiritual. . . .

In reality, Eliot had read very little of the men Clarke recommended to him, but he had developed a crude philosophy of life around the concepts of faith, and truth, and duty. He had only a smattering of Goethe, and Kant, and Fichte, but he had gained from them the ideal of self-development through the search for truth and the performance of duty. He had established a philosophical foundation for his life that the rationalism of Unitarianism had somehow deprived him and his fellows of. The patronizing, and in some ways, self-satisfied, Clarke had feared injuring Eliot, by leading him into unknown realms; but Eliot was never caught in the snares that were to confound Clarke, William Henry Channing, and Margaret Fuller. While Transcendentalism led Clarke to the free church movement; Channing to associationism and socialism and eventually to England; and Margaret Fuller to Italy, it led Eliot to St. Louis. Eliot did not like the stony soil of Boston, but he never lost his footing. He did not lose sight of his ministry. By 1834 he had decided that the soil of the Mississippi Valley was more fertile, and he headed west to plant Christian institutions.

William Greenleaf Eliot circa 1835
(Courtesy Washington University Archives)

CHAPTER I
"ST. LOUIS, NEAR ALTON"

". . . if I come I come to remain, and to lay my ashes in the Valley of the Mississippi."

On November 27, 1834, William Greenleaf Eliot saw St. Louis for the first time. We may imagine him leaning against the rail of the riverboat which had carried him on the last leg of the long westward journey, straining for his first glimpse of the place, then little more than a frontier town in what was considered the far west.

Except for his deep, soulful eyes, he was an unimpressive figure. Youthful — he had celebrated his twenty-third birthday in early August — and slight of stature, it seems doubtful he made much of an impression on any who shared his journey, still more doubtful that he expressed to any of them either his doubts about himself or his dreams about the little city of 7000 or so which he intended, even then, to make the locus of his life's work. St. Louis lay on the west bank of the Mississippi River, a little south of where it was joined by the Missouri and Illinois Rivers, and also a little south of the then more prominent river town of Alton, Illinois. Three years before, while working in the Post Office in Washington, D.C., his family home, Eliot had seen letters addressed to "St. Louis, near Alton." Intrigued, he had examined maps of the region, and of the whole Mississippi Valley. Very likely William Eliot foresaw much of what St. Louis would become, though almost certainly the reality surpassed his visions. Centrally located in what would become America's bread-basket, the gateway to what was then and would be for some time the Wild West, ideally situated as a major port along the network of riverways which were more important for commerce than the railways until later in the century, St. Louis was destined for greatness. William Eliot may have had some inkling of all this, but with his modesty of character it seems unlikely that he foresaw the place he would take in the building of what would become in his lifetime the largest inland city of the United States.

Of course we cannot know his thoughts as he saw St. Louis for the first time. We may imagine it to have been as unimpressive as he, and perhaps Eliot's doubts overwhelmed his dreams as the riverboat neared the landing. Among the crowd gathered on the levy, he picked out the face of Christopher Rhodes, who had interviewed him at the Divinity School in Cambridge a few months before. Immediately upon his arrival, Rhodes took him to the office of another gentleman, James Smith. These two were the welcoming party. Eliot later named a son after Christopher Rhodes and a boys' Academy after James Smith. These men would become two of his closest friends and strongest supporters in the years of great accomplishment that lay ahead. But at this time they were merely two new acquaintancs and Eliot only a fledgling minister, a youth taking his first assignment. Would he be adequate even to the tiny task which lay immediately before him, to build a community of Unitarian Christian faith here in the west?

Perhaps the indecision which he had expressed several months earlier to his friend James Freeman Clarke returned momentarily. Clarke had graduated from the Divinity School a year before Eliot and had similarly proceeded westward, to Louisville (though, like virtually all of the Unitarian — and other — seminarians who went west to test their wings, Clarke returned to the east after only a few years. He settled in the Boston area, wrote and published widely, and became one of the major leaders of the relatively new denomination.) As early as September of 1833 Eliot had written to Clarke in Louisville, saying ". . . I wish you would give me the benefit of your experience as much as you can. I feel as if the West or the South will be my sphere of action. . . ." On October 12, 1833, he wrote:

> I wish you would in your next letter tell me something . . . of what the prospect in the West *is* for us young Unitarian Preachers. Is it, on the whole, a good field for useful labor? It is not a question of Curiosity. I hear that, at St. Louis, a parish is getting together, is it true; and what about it?

And on February 7, 1834, in another letter to Clarke, he raised the subject yet again:

> . . . St. Louis is very far. But, says the better and more heroic voice, "The mind is its own place." That's poetry, says selfishness. Then let the Christian's life be a poem. "You will do much good there," says Philanthropy. But selfishness is sharp-sighted, "Can you not do good here also, and at the same time be more happy?" It is humble, too, "Why assume so much to yourself, others could do better than you."
> . . . But says the self-sacrificing spirit, "if I do not go, nobody will. Besides, how noble it is to work for God's glory, and to do your part towards regenerating the soul of man! You may be the means of rearing up a generation of Christians where Infidels now stand! And what matter is it whether the few years of life are spent in cities or in wilderness, in a court or among boors, in the East or in the West?" "You are becoming very visionary," says selfishness. James, I am doubtful — yet very decided I must *know* more: what is the prospect for success? what the character of the people? the probable number of Unitarians to begin with, the peculiar discouragements, etc. Can you not let me know this and all else that you longed to know before you went out. But tell me this. Say decidedly to me, "You can succeed. You have the *requisite ability*." And, if I know myself, I will come. "The *requisite ability*". . . . *Speak candidly*. . . .
> The self-sacrifice — though it sometimes comes over me like a cold hand on the heart — in general seems *nothing at all*. My spirit, and all that is within me revolts from a self-seeking ministry of the Gospel. I do not wish to live *here*, I will not do so. I think I will not. But there are other places besides St. Louis — and I wish you to get for me information as to the real prospect there. Are they desirous to form a parish? Let them know in some way that a youngster is ready to come there to live, and spend his life among them, if they will provide food and lodging: for if I come I come to remain, and to lay my ashes in the Valley of the Mississippi.

His concluding sentence sounds like mere youthful rhetoric, but despite great temptations over the years to leave St. Louis, Eliot remained faithful to this pledge, and it rings now with the resonance of true prophecy: "If I come I come to remain, and to lay my ashes in the Valley of the Mississippi."

But this letter is interesting for other reasons as well. In it are many of the familiar expressions and concerns of youth. He asks twice for reassurance that he has the "requisite ability" and underlines the words both times. He is resolute and indecisive in the same breath: "I do not wish to live here [in Boston], I will not do so. I think I will not."

Young Eliot's insecurities may have been compounded in his experiences at Harvard's Divinity School and the community which surrounded it. Unlike many of his classmates and friends there, he had not attended Harvard as an undergraduate. (Eliot's grandfather, the Rev. Andrew Eliot, 1718–1778, was the first member of the family to graduate from Harvard, in 1737, and many others, of course, followed in his footsteps. But William attended Columbian College, a Baptist school in Washington, D.C., where his family was then living and from which he was graduated in 1830.)

He worked for a year as an assistant clerk in the chief examiner's room at the Postal Department in Washington before enrolling in the Harvard Divinity School in the fall of 1831. At Cambridge he formed what was to be a lifelong friendship with James Freeman Clarke. Through Clarke he became acquainted with Margaret Fuller and others of that elite intellectual group which met frequently to discuss literature and philosophy, mostly German, and who would be among the leaders of the Transcendentalist movement. The practical-minded Eliot seems to have existed on the fringes of this group because of his friendship with Clarke, but he was never really part of it, socially or intellectually.

Late in his life Eliot related an incident which occurred at this time which must have made a deep impression to be remembered some fifty years later: He was walking across Boston Common one day with Margaret Fuller, who possessed one of the finest minds in America, with an ego and tongue to match. He made some self-deprecating remarks about his intellectual capacities, obviously hoping to elicit some words of encouragement from her: "My work must be done with small capital; I cannot originate, but must work with the tools others put within my reach: not a prophet but an interpreter." However, instead of the sympathetic response he had hoped for, Fuller merely said, "How few people judge themselves so rightly as you do." Eliot said that he had not expected "such hearty concurrence" and "subsided."

So Eliot did not find himself in the social or intellectual circles of Boston, but he did find a lifelong fiend in James Freeman Clarke. Eliot's letters to Clarke over the years are unusually intimate and open; they provide some of the most revelatory glimpses into the inner man. In this respect they are generally superior even to the journal, or Notebooks, which Eliot kept at times during his life.

From New Bedford in August of 1833, Eliot had written to Clarke, saying, "I predict that the correspondence now commenced shall end only with the lives [sic] of one of us." In the same letter he went on to say,

> I think that many hours will soon come in which a friend's voice would soothe, and when it would be pleasant to speak in a friend's ear — but such a friend you cannot have near you. I do not know how far the want can be supplied by a distant one, but wilt thou not try? I can at least sympathize, I hope, with every feeling you can have; and I am sure I should never misunderstand any thing you can write. Perhaps the greatest pleasure of friendship arises from this, that one is not *misunderstood* as by ordinary acquaintance; we have talked of that — and you may be satisfied that I shall be, at least in this, true. Ergo, as you would speak, write; and I will read, as if I had *heard*.

On September 17, 1834, in another letter to Clarke, from Washington, D.C., Eliot said, "My letters to you are *in loco journal* and are better pictures of my

21

thoughts than anything I write besides." This is generally true, though Eliot did make periodic attempts at keeping a regular journal.

There are ten Notebooks — a combination of diary, workbook and scrapbook — which comprise what we have of Eliot's journal. The first was begun in November of 1847 when Eliot was 36; the last ends in 1877, about ten years before his death. And there are gaps of months and even years within and among them. So the Notebooks are a source both of endless fascination and continual frustration to the scholar. The frustration is compounded by the fact that Eliot's daughter-in-law, Charlotte (mother of the poet, T. S. Eliot), in the process of writing a biography, permanently "edited" the Notebooks by removing several pages which she found objectionable.

Relative to the significance of his life and accomplishment, William Greenleaf Eliot has not received anywhere near the recognition either of the scholar or of the general public which he deserves. In a city which remembers its history better than most, frequent reference is made to some of Eliot's friends such as Eads, Shaw, Yeatman and others, all of whom would, I believe, consider it very strange that they are remembered better than the minister who arrived on that November day in 1834 and who over the next half-century marked the building of one of the great cities of America with the stamp of his character. The major private university in that city, founded mainly by him and originally named for him, did not have even a memorial plaque in his honor until 1953, when on the occasion of the Centennial of Washington University, one was placed there by action of members of the First Unitarian Church of St. Louis. (See Appendix III.)

But it is not by accident that Eliot's name and life have been to a considerable extent effaced from memory. If he had had what was apparently his authentic wish and desire, we would not remember him at all, nor possess even the relatively few documents we have from his own hand to read and study. Indeed, this present work represents an outright defiance of his explicit instruction and request, written out and many times reiterated, that no biography or even eulogy be written. Among the instructions he left to his family and executors were these:

> I earnestly *request* that no Memorial window or Tablet or Bust shall be placed in the Church of the Messiah or any other public place. . . I hope that this *request,* which I make an injunction so far as in me lies, will be strictly complied with. . . . I need hardly say that I hope no "biography" or memorial book will be attempted. "Requiescam in pace." What is worth remembering will take care of itself and in human records the better part of truth is silence.

These instructions are no affectation. They are in harmony with the personal modesty Eliot displayed consistently throughout his life. At times his desire to minimize or even hide his personal responsibility for achievements in which he must have taken justifiable pride seems almost incomprehensible. We shall discuss several examples of this personal modesty — a characteristic not necessarily common among men of strong purpose and high achievement — in hopes that we might be in a better position to understand it.

Let us now, for contrast, consider another clergyman of the same period, also a man of distinction and accomplishment, a man whose beliefs and values parallel Eliot's in many respects, yet who seems almost his exact opposite because they differed so markedly in this one way, a man as immodest as Eliot was self-effacing. The man is Henry Ward Beecher, an early adept of the modern art of self-promotion.

They were almost exact contemporaries, and Beecher is now as famous as Eliot is obscure. Like Eliot, Beecher began his career in the west, but soon realized that only the east could satisfy his need for public notice and popular success. In his famous Plymouth Church in Brooklyn he built a lofty platform, more a runway than a pulpit, from which he commanded the attention of the enthralled thousands who came as much to be entertained as edified. In the course of teaching Christ, Beecher celebrated himself in a manner which fellow-Brooklynite Walt Whitman might applaud and a style which the Madison Avenue of the next century could appreciate. When Beecher's brother Tom appeared on the platform one Sunday in his brother's place, many of the disappointed parishioners started leaving the church. Tom regaled them by pretending to announce: "Those who came to worship God may remain, those who came to worship Henry Ward Beecher may depart." Beecher was a politician of the pulpit. He gained influence by the power of his personality, and he used that influence as widely and publicly as he was able.

To Beecher, Eliot stands in stark contrast. They had similar gifts and similar goals but different egos. If Beecher celebrated himself, Eliot denied himself. The one sought publicity, the other shunned it. For Beecher the pulpit — and the preacher who filled it — was the center of the church; for Eliot the center of the church was the communion table. This last is more than a symbolic statement of the difference between them. Eliot sought to lead a life of consecration. This old-fashioned word is the only one that fits. He really did seek to live as a servant of Christ.

In a notebook which Eliot used during his last year at the Divinity School he had written: "I must learn to preach not myself but Christ." Whether his own or borrowed from one of his teachers, this was a phrase he reiterated throughout his life. (He repeated it to his oldest son, Thomas Lamb Eliot, upon his graduation from the Harvard Divinity School years later, in a list of fatherly and professional advice: "Preach Christ," he wrote, "not T. L. E.") In that notebook from his last year in the seminary, on August 24, 1834, Eliot had written:

> . . . I regard my preaching for the last and next two months as a continual uphill work. When I get to St. Louis out of the reach of Friends, it will be better. How rejoiced I am that I am to be removed from all I love or who love me — for there I shall be more able to forget myself in my duties, which *now* I am not permitted to do. I am tired of congratulations of having "acquitted *myself* well" — is that the object of my mission? No. I must forget myself, and die in the flesh, or I shall never live in Christ.

And to his friend Clarke a few weeks later, he wrote: "A minister, to do his duty, must be in a situation where he is permitted to do his best without praise, where he may forget himself in his work."

To our age, which is in thrall to the doctrines and dogmas of self-esteem and self-assertion, such sentiments as these may seem odd indeed, but we cannot hope to understand Eliot without understanding them. The key to this understanding may well lie in the gospel passage: "If any man would come after me, let him deny himself and take up his cross and follow me. For whoever would save his life will lose it, and whoever loses his life for my sake will find it."

When Eliot stood at the rail of the steamboat on that chilly November day in 1834, he saw not what must have been the rather unimpressive visage of a little frontier river town but the locus of his life's work, his vocation. He saw not only the place where he would take up his profession but where he would live his life. He had come not to be served but to serve, not to be ministered unto but to minister, to lose his life in service to Christ and to man and thereby to find it. Such expressions as these were not empty pieties to him but living realities.

Like his Puritan forbears, William Greenleaf Eliot saw life not in terms of satisfactions but of duties. That which was labelled duty took on almost a hallowed quality for him. To discover one's duty and then to do it, that was the purpose of life, and Eliot would teach this lesson even more by example than by preachment. Of the two elements by far the harder task was to discover what duty required, for once it became clear what duty was, there was not the least question that one should and would set upon doing it, no matter how arduous the task nor how great the personal sacrifice it entailed. If this attitude seems strange or artificial to us today, it is as much a judgement upon ourselves as upon him and the Puritan heritage which he embodied.

Eliot would not have gone to St. Louis without a sense of the call of duty, and once this was clear, all the hesitancy reflected in his early letters to Clarke and all the youthful indecision disappeared. He came, and he came to stay. Here was where the path of duty led, and despite the calls and the strong temptations to return to the east, calls that held (as they did for Beecher and for many others) the certain promise of ease and comfort, material gain, expanded influence, perhaps fame — even in at least one instance which we shall discuss in detail, a possible claim to higher duty — none would sway him from what appears to have been for him a consecrated course.

The initial terms of his contract were for the trial period of a year, but once he arrived there was never again any mention of a trial, or for that matter of a contract. He was offered as compensation for his year's labor "board, loadging [sic] and the blessings of God."

Upwards of a hundred or more crowded into Elihu Shepherd's school rooms across from the Court House to hear Eliot's first sermon the Sunday after his arrival. Shortly thereafter, larger quarters were sought even as the numbers in the congregation dwindled. No doubt there were many curiosity-seekers among the early crowds, and these of course disappeared once the novelty had worn off. But there was more to it. The Unitarians (even then) were regarded by many as infidels, and at least some people came with the expectation of hearing Christianity ridiculed and the life of faith decried. To such as these the youthful Eliot could not have been a greater disappointment. He was at pains in his early sermons to give no comfort to those who associated Unitarianism with atheism or deism. What is remarkable is how controversial the church was even when represented by so conservative a radical as Eliot was.

In later years Eliot reported that the smallest congregation to which he preached in those early years numbered eight, on "a very pleasant day in March, 1835." But on another Sunday in that first year he declined to preach at all when there was, he said, "but one person present besides himself and the sexton, and that one was the gentleman with whom he lived." Eliot related stories and statistics like this in later years, I suspect, largely to give encouragement to Unitarian churches (many of which he helped to organize) struggling through their own early years. By the time he talked in this way about its history his church had grown to be one of the largest and most influential in the west. However, his letters to the American Unitarian Association back in Boston (which was providing a small amount of financial support for the St. Louis endeavor and from whom he sought additional funds) during those same early years reflect only success and enthusiasm. Eliot was no fool, especially when it came to money. Whatever the exact and actual circumstances of what others may have considered an experiment, it is clear that Eliot himself was never uncertain of ultimate success.

The decision to build a church building seems to have been influenced at least in part by the difficulty in obtaining a suitable hall. Shepherd's school rooms having proved, at least initially, to be too small, the church had got the loan of the Court House, where Eliot preached several Sundays. But a group of lawyers, members of more orthodox churches, drew up a petition to eject the Unitarians from the Court House, and their efforts succeeded. When the Unitarians applied

First church building, Northwest corner of Fourth and Pine
Dedicated October 29, 1837
(*Courtesy First Unitarian Church Archives*)

for the use of City Hall, which had been used for this purpose by others in the past, they were similarly denied.

On January 26, 1835, the First Congregational Society of St. Louis was formally organized. Seventeen people signed the Membership Book initially, the first name being that of William Greenleaf Eliot. Eliot was in Boston that May for the Annual Meeting of the American Unitarian Association, at which he was already pleading the cause of expansion in the west. "We want *preachers,*" he told the gentlemen gathered in the Berry Street Church vestry, and continued:

> I do not speak of great talent; we can do without that; but without men of disinterested, persevering self-devotion we cannot do. . . . We need chiefly good sense and devoted love of Christ. Our other want is sympathy, aid and encouragement from our brethren of the East. . . . In the days of our small things, give us from your abundance, and we may soon be able to return to you four-fold.

The people of Boston would become accustomed to hearing such appeals from Mr. Eliot over the coming years, and — as he would often remind them — he was better than his word. He was in Boston this time principally to raise funds for the church building in St. Louis. Through personal appeals and by preaching on Sundays and taking contributions he brought back $3000 toward the cost of the church's first permanent home, a simple Doric temple located at the northwest corner of Fourth and Pine Streets, which cost in all $17,000. The little congregation incurred a substantial debt to complete it.

The church was dedicated on October 29, 1837. In his dedication sermon Eliot emphasized the Christian character of Unitarianism: "We are here, brethren, in God's name, as Christians; acknowledging Jesus Christ as our Lord and Master, we come to consecrate this house; to dedicate it to his father and our father, to his God and our God." The reason for this emphasis, especially on so prominent and public an occasion, was that Eliot knew that for many, Unitarianism implied unconventional religion, or irreligion. "We have been asked, even in this city," he said,

> by those who are accounted intelligent men, whether there is any difference between a Unitarian and a Deist, and not a few have expressed surprise, when they heard the name of Christ spoken in our prayers. It is needful for us, often and publicly, to proclaim that we believe in Christ, or we fail of obtaining credit for belonging to the Christian family. . . .

Eliot's Unitarianism was not notably conservative for its time, and it is perhaps surprising to realize that the Unitarian faith that now sounds so orthodox to us was considered radical then. In his sermon Eliot listed six ends to which his church was dedicated, only the last of which seems to distinguish the church substantially from many others. The church was dedicated, Eliot said:

First, to the worship of Almighty God;

Second, to Jesus Christ;

Third, to the teaching of the Holy Scriptures;

Fourth, to the spiritual life, to faith, to religion in its essential spirit;

Fifth, to the teaching and practice of morality;

Sixth, and finally, he said:

> We dedicate this house to *Religious Freedom.* . . . We would carefully avoid putting any restraint upon men's consciences. Accordingly, we have given to this church the name Congregational, rather than Unitarian, because we do not wish to restrain men, even by a word. . . . This church is not pledged to support Unitarianism, but Christianity, and all Christians are welcome here. According to the same principle, we acknowledge the authority of no creed but the Bible. The New Testament is itself our articles of faith and rules of discipline.

This was Unitarian Christianity as Eliot had heard it preached by William Ellery Channing, the founder of American Unitarianism, in the Federal Street

Church in Boston, where Eliot had been ordained (as an Evangelist, a point he always emphasized), and as it was taught in the Divinity School in Cambridge. It would be the Unitarianism preached by Eliot to the end of his life, even though by that time the Unitarian denomination itself would be divided into more conservative and more radical wings, and Eliot would publicly express his sense of estrangement from the radicals. But all this lay far in the future. For now his perspective was that of a young man, not yet in his thirtieth year, anxious to make a success of a little church in a distant, almost unknown city of the west.

Among the luxuries he had left behind were the libraries and other sources of intellectual stimulation of the older eastern cities. This was something he frequently lamented in his letters to Clarke, and Clarke, no doubt motivated by similar feelings, had initiated a journal called *The Western Messenger,* to which Eliot was a frequent contributor. Many of the theological articles which Eliot and the other western ministers contributed to the *Messenger's* pages were reworkings of sermons, but the range of topics covered in its pages was wide and reflected practical as well as philosophical concerns, and most were of general interest even though dedicated to the particular concerns of the west. All the early issues of the *Western Messenger* have one or more articles by Eliot in them, although in some cases the authorship is uncertain since they are sometimes unsigned or only initialed. Of particular interest is a "Letter on Mobs," written by Eliot, from Baltimore, and published in the third issue of the *Messenger* in September of 1835:

> . . . Knowing as I do, the excited, boiling feelings, universal at the south, I would make any degree of effort, to induce emancipators to be still. Their zeal is wholly without knowledge; they know nothing of the true difficulties of the case, or they would not speak and act as they do. If all the non-slaveholding States should unite in one voice, and rise up as one man, they could do nothing to help the slaves of the south. It is utterly impossible to induce the southerners to hear or think of such interferences, without anger. Even in Virginia, where slavery is not loved, where they would gladly be rid of it, there is a feeling of resentment throughout her borders, against "northern incendiaries," as they are here termed. The wise and good of that State are now remonstrating publicly with the north, and calling upon them to join, in hushing the voice of those who will soon work disunion, but the multitude cannot wish to remonstrate, and are full of bitterness. We would say to these erring philanthropists, "for God's sake, desist; for liberty's sake, for your country's sake! You may work disunion, for the southern States at this hour, almost desire it, and *do not* fear it. You may make, nay, are making the bondage of the slave tenfold more severe than it ever was before. You are exciting the most deadly feeling of hostility against the free blacks, and may bring about them, general massacre throughout the south. But you can do no good by your most earnest efforts. If you are true Christians, and true philanthropists, be silent now, and wait for God's time. It will soon come. Why expect to remove mountains in an hour?" Would to God, our voice could reach them. But there is fear that they will not rest, till their own eyes rest upon the ruin they are like to work. The experiment will never be tried, of immediate, general emancipation, but many terrible days and nights of bloodshed, may devastate our cities.

Thus we may see that the pages of the *Western Messenger* contained not only abstract theological discourse but references to the great moral and practical issues of the time. And in this letter, too, we have an early outline of Eliot's thinking about the great issue of his time, the preliminary form of his position as a "gradual emancipationist." Confident of the moral progress of mankind under God's guidance, Eliot sought the ultimate abolishment of the evil of slavery while avoiding the equal or greater evils of disunion and war. This position, though it was frequently misrepresented and misunderstood by others, he would hold consistently and firmly through all the difficult and anguished years that lay ahead.

He would stand his moral ground in the public every bit as much as the private sphere.

It is perhaps just as well that the youth of the 1830s could not forsee the St. Louis and the United States of the 1860s.

In all, the burdens of the future would be great. The path which he had chosen, the path which duty decreed, was a demanding one: morally, spiritually — and physically. Eliot possessed abundant strength of character, but he was small and even somewhat frail physically. His journals are punctuated with references to minor disabilities, headaches, weakness, fatigue.

On several occasions during the years of his ministry, Eliot received formal letters signed by a number of his parishioners expressing concern about the state of his health and encouraging him to periods of rest and relaxation. Eliot did travel from St. Louis on several occasions, but many, if not most, of these trips were less vacations, although he sometimes referred to them as such, than new opportunities for evangelism. In September of 1849, for example, Eliot left St. Louis on an "indefinite excursion." "My mind must have entire relief from ordinary cares in preparation for the winter's campaign," he wrote in his journal at Tremont, Illinois — and then went on to note that he had been there for "four days, Preached five times, and on Sunday afternoon organized a church. . . ."

This was a fairly typical exercise. Even before the St. Louis church was firmly established, Eliot involved himself in the development of Unitarian churches in other western communities, the first in Alton, Illinois, where a society (which did not survive) was organized in 1836. Over the years Eliot's missionary ventures took him as far south as New Orleans and as far north as Milwaukee. He considered himself an emissary to a wide territory, and he appeared regularly at the annual meetings of the American Unitarian Association held in Boston in May each year at the time of the General Elections, to plead the cause of the west.

Even on his three extended journeys to Europe, Eliot could not entirely abandon his natural inclinations. A letter back to the Association during one of these trips indicates that he was involved in discussions concerning the establishment of a Unitarian church in Paris!

It was following his return from the first of these European trips, in 1847, that Eliot commenced his journal, the ten Notebooks referred to earlier, which are the most important single source of primary materials available to Eliot scholars. Given his almost obsessive modesty, one might reasonably wonder why he desired to keep such a record and, despite the gaps of months and even years in them, hoped to keep as full a record as possible.

One reason for keeping them, of course, was practical. The Notebooks are not merely a record of his activity but also a place for drafting letters and jotting down sermon ideas and pasting scraps of potentially useful information from newspapers and elsewhere. In other words the Notebooks are a combination journal, workbook and scrapbook.

But I believe there is a more significant reason why Eliot kept a journal, which is suggested by the time he began keeping it. He commenced his journal in 1847 immediately following a crucial life and career decision, a decision to reject an invitation to return to the east, to Boston, to a position of some prominence. But he declined, despite the urgings of friends and colleagues and most significant of all against the stated wishes of his father, which were expressed in the strongest of terms. No Eliot lightly defied the wishes of his parents.

I believe that the journal being undertaken just at this point in his life reflects in major part Eliot's need to justify his decision to remain in St. Louis and reaffirm the original commitment he had made to his adopted home — more simply, the need to justify his life. That life must be justified by accomplishment was an unquestioned article of the Eliot family credo. (The family crest, in one version, includes the motto, "Fac et Tac," which was loosely translated, "Shut up and work.") But even accomplishment by itself was insufficient; it must be right accomplishment, good work.

Eliot never doubted that his chosen profession was the highest calling to which a man could aspire. He accepted only reluctantly the fact that not all of his sons chose the ministry for their life's work. His oldest son, Thomas Lamb Eliot (born October 13, 1841) emulated his father's life and work to an almost eerie degree, re-creating in the new west — in Portland, Oregon — a ministry that was almost the mirror image of that of his father in St. Louis, the west of a generation earlier. (Thom's church in Portland was named The Church of Our Father, and there is reason to wonder whether someone other than the Heavenly Father might have been subconsciously intended. And The Portland church was later served by *Thomas'* son, William Greenleaf Eliot, Jr.) Of the three other sons who reached adulthood, only the youngest, Christopher Rhodes Eliot (born January 20, 1856) went into the ministry, serving a distinguished career in the Boston area and siring, among other children, a future President of the American Unitarian Association, Frederick May Eliot. Some of the correspondence between Eliot and his children — particularly that between him and Thomas — has been preserved, and it is reflective of an intimate, caring and involved family. Generational conflict seems to have been non-existent, and one is surprised by the almost effusive emotion in some of these letters. It seems to have been a warm, deeply-bonded and affectionate family and home. The evidence suggests the kind of family typically described as, and today often castigated for being, patriarchal and traditional. It was no doubt both.

Eliot married a cousin, Abby Adams Cranch, in June of 1837. (Eliot's father, incidentally, had also married a cousin.) Abby's father was a District Court judge in Washington, D.C., where the wedding was held, and she knew that this marriage meant she would leave behind the comforts of the urban and urbane east for the privations of the primitive west. (See Appendix I for Abby's impressions of the St. Louis of this period as she remembered them in 1895.)

Mrs. Eliot was obviously a woman of strong character and equally sturdy constitution. She bore 14 children, of whom only five survived to full maturity, although two of the girls, including Eliot's beloved first-born, Mary (for whom Mary Institute would later be named), lived into their teens, only serving to make more painful and tragic their loss. Twenty years old at the time of her marriage, six years younger than her husband, Abby outlived him by 21 years and died in St. Louis on October 20, 1908, at age 91. Their most famous grandchild, the poet T. S. Eliot, in a reflection upon his own childhood in St. Louis, once provided a perspective on the nature of the Eliot family; speaking to a large St. Louis audience in 1953, he said:

> I never knew my grandfather; he died a year before my birth. But I was brought up to be very much aware of him: so much so, that as a child I thought of him as still head of the family — a ruler for whom *in absentia* my grandmother stood as vicegerent. The standard of conduct was that which my grandfather had set; our moral judgements, our decisions between duty and self-indulgence, were taken as if, like Moses, he had brought down tables of the Law, any deviation from which would be sinful. Not the least of these laws, which included injunctions still more than prohibitions, was the Law of Public Service: it is no doubt owing to the impress of this law upon my infant mind that, like other members of my family, I have felt, ever since I passed beyond my early irresponsible years, an uncomfortable and very inconvenient obligation to serve upon committees. This original Law of Public Service operated especially in three areas: the Church, the City, and the University. The Church meant, for us, the Unitarian Church of the Messiah, then

situated in Locust Street . . .; the City was St. Louis — the utmost outskirts of which touched on Forest Park, terminus of the Olive Street streetcars, and to me, as a child, the beginning of the Wild West; the University was Washington University, then housed in a modest building in lower Washington Avenue. These were the symbols of Religion, the Community, and Education: and I think it is a very good beginning for any child, to be brought up to reverence such institutions, and to be taught that personal and selfish aims should be subordinated to the general good which they represent. . . .

The creation of two of these symbols — the Church and the University — and major contributions toward the creation of the character of the third constitute the major part of William Greenleaf Eliot's accomplishment, the justification of his life. The various "laws" to which the poet refers above, which Eliot embodied and instilled in his family, were simply the tradition he had inherited from his Puritan ancestry. They represent nothing extraordinary except in the seriousness with which they were taken and the degree to which they were followed. They contained the best of the Puritan heritage, though not without the consequence of occasionally revealing the flaws in Puritanism. The "Law of Public Service," to which the poet makes special reference, was, like all the Eliot admonitions, a *divine* command. To the Puritan, one's service to humanity was more than simply an aspect of one's obligation to God; the one was an intimate part of the other, for God was not distant but ever-present, not a mighty abstraction but a living reality, and one served Him in fear and trembling, though also in confidence of His actual participation in every day of one's life.

William Greenleaf Eliot was one of the best and purest examples of what Daniel Howe has labelled, in a fine book, "The Unitarian Conscience." Puritan moralism was a key element in 19th century Unitarianism. This fact may come as a surprise to those familiar only with Unitarianism in its contemporary form which has substituted for the earlier moral absolutism an almost absolute moral relativity, but such is the case. Even so, in other respects as well, 20th century Unitarianism has turned the 19th century on its head. The "faith once given to the Saints" from the lips of William Ellery Channing, the founder of American Unitarianism, was God-centered, Christ-saturated, simple and sentimental. Its object was personal virtue. As Howe observes,

> The Unitarian moralists continued in the proud tradition of Puritan moralism that Ralph Barton Perry so well summed up: "The Puritan held, incredible as it may now seem, that morals are more important than athletics, business, or art. He held that to achieve a controlling will by which to conform one's life to what one conceives to be the way of righteousness is the one thing most profoundly needful. Or rather, he held that athletics, business, and art should be judged by conscience, and approved only so long as they form parts of that good life — that orderly and integral life, of the person or of the society — which must be founded on virtue."

William Greenleaf Eliot came to St. Louis with youthful idealism, religious vision, and moral passion. The path of duty was, to him, divinely ordained. To the social, economic and moral anarchy of the west he brought the Unitarian conscience, born of his Puritan ancestry and heritage. St. Louis would be his "city set on a hill," and its history would be marked by his influence.

As I have suggested earlier, the decisive crisis in his life came, not in 1834 with his initial call to St. Louis, but in 1847, with a call to return east to Boston. Many of his generation, like him, answered first calls to the west, bringing youthful exuberance to new churches and cities. But almost all returned within a few years to the comfortable homes, the libraries and culture, of the east. And, after a dozen years in St. Louis, having successfully launched a new church,

30

William Greenleaf Eliot received a call to return to Boston under the most favorable circumstances.

In September of 1846, finally responding to the urgings of members of his congregation who recognized the signs of overwork in their pastor, Eliot left St. Louis for an extended time. The pulpit was filled in his absence by the Rev. William O. White. In February of 1847, Eliot sailed for Europe via the good ship *St. Nicholas,* accompanied by his good friend and parishioner, William Glasgow. They made the grand tour. Eliot was 35 years old.

In his absence he was elected to head the American Unitarian Association.

In Paris in early June Eliot received a letter from his father giving the details. The American Unitarian Association in 1847 was a very different organization than the denomination today. Basically it was a clergyman's club which gathered in Boston each May, at the time of the Massachusetts General Elections. The Association's major work was the publishing of tracts, mostly sermons by the gentlemen there gathered. The Association's executive was called the Secretary, and it was this office to which Eliot was elected, *in absentia,* as his father's letter explained, by a two-thirds majority on the first ballot, "and," his father said, "I don't know how the Unitarian clergy could have paid you a higher compliment — the salary they voted to be two thousand dollars." The letter went on to proclaim the benefits of Boston and the declaration: "You would *fill the very place you were made for."* Eliot, Senior, argued not just the suitability of the office to his son's talents, but, more significant in his own mind, his son's duty to his family, not to continue to expose them to the difficult and unhealthful life in St. Louis, with its lack of educational and cultural opportunities, or even for that matter adequate sewage systems. This was as strong a letter as any Eliot could write or receive, arguing as it did the path of duty.

Eliot did not decide immediately upon whether to accept the position. After his return from Europe in September, he stayed in the east, and undoubtedly there were discussions on the matter not only with Abby (who along with the children had been staying with her family in Washington during her husband's absence) but with his father.

Finally, on October 1, Eliot wrote a letter declining the appointment. The reasons for his refusal, he said, "are in some degree of a personal nature, and I need not here account them, but they are to my mind quite conclusive, and leave no room for doubt with regard to my duty."

The Minutes of a Special Meeting of the American Unitarian Association held on October 21 to discuss Eliot's decision note that he declined "from a conviction of duty growing out of his peculiar relation to the church in St. Louis."

On November 9, 1847, Eliot arrived back in St. Louis and immediately commenced his journal. The first entry indicates that on his return he went first to the house of Mr. Wayman Crow, a prominent member of his congregation.

On the following Sunday, November 14, he preached to a very full church on the text, "one thing is needful." The following Tuesday he opened his journal and wrote:

> Certainly my only motive in returning to St. Louis is that of duty; and if there had been reasonable prospect of any good minister for them who would devote himself to them, I should have remained in Boston. The position offered to me there is very honorable and might be made very influential, and if I could have fulfilled its duties well I might have placed myself at the head of the denomination and developed capacities in the Unitarian body, of which no one now has adequate knowledge. . . . There is a wonderful attraction in the very air of Boston and Cambridge.

He concluded this entry by saying that "duty was (the) deciding motive and to say truth I have felt the sacrifice very deeply."

MISCELLANY, 1834–1848

"A minister, to do his duty, must be in a situation where he is permitted to do his best without praise, where he may forget himself in his work."
— *WGE in letter to James Freeman Clarke (JFC), September 17, 1834*

*　　　*　　　*

"Were you ever in Pittsburgh? Then congratulate yourself, for you have escaped the nastiest place in creation."
— *WGE, from Pittsburgh, to JFC, October 16, 1834*

*　　　*　　　*

"Why do we live? That we may learn to live well. Time is the threshold of eternity. . . . A long life well spent is not too much.

"To encourage the hope that the soul may be born again out of the darkness of gross sin and worldly-minded unbelief, into the light of holiness and faith, by a sudden effort, called conversion, may increase the number of the visible church of Christ, but it is not and cannot come to good. It is against nature, and cannot be true. . . .

"We ourselves must do this work [of salvation]. One man cannot repent for another nor reform for another. God will help us in the work, but he will not do it for us. Christ will guide us by his truth, and encourage us by his example, but he will not give us his righteousness as a cloak to cover over our sins. Under God and through Christ, we must save ourselves. By the action of our own minds we must learn to perceive the truth, and supply it to ourselves. Our own hearts must feel. Our spiritual nature must, by our own effort, be unfolded and established, through faith in goodness, in eternity, in Christ and in God. We must act for ourselves, according to our own consciences, independently; not in crowds, not as the creatures of circumstances, but thoughtfully, as those who shall render an account. The work of salvation is one of self-searching, self-direction, self-sacrifice. If we find it hard, it must nevertheless be done. If we need assistance, it cannot come from man, but from God."
— *from "Salvation Not Easily Obtained" by WGE,* Western Messenger, *May, 1836*

*　　　*　　　*

"For myself, I would not leave the corner that I now occupy for the best pulpit in Boston. To one who enters into the western spirit and realizes the truth as to the future greatness of this valley, there is much to fascinate, and compensate for privations and loneliness."
— *WGE to C. Briggs, July 13, 1836*

*　　　*　　　*

"If any religion ever prospers in the West, it must be one at the same time rational and fervent, for men both reason and feel strongly there; it must at the same time be free from bigotry and full of zeal; and such is our [Unitarian] faith when truly understood."
— *WGE, May, 1838*

". . . I am bound to no theory and disdain all systems: Yet I am more Orthodox than when we knew each other, and still going in that direction. I bind myself more and more to Jesus Christ, and accord him more and more authority and honor."

— *WGE to JFC, November 15, 1840*

* * *

"The Unitarian Church is represented in this remote place [St. Louis], as in most other parts of America, by a gentleman of great worth and excellence. The poor have good reason to remember and bless it; for it befriends them, and aids the cause of rational education, without any sectarian or selfish views. It is liberal in all its actions; of kind construction; and of wide benevolence."

— *Charles Dickens in his* American Notes, *Chapter 12 (1843)*

* * *

"Eleven years — think of that — Eleven years and more, since I came to this city: then so fresh and zealous and strong-hearted, and now with the resolution of principle as the sole substitute for the involuntary, over-flowing impulses of the new worker. There are few persons who have worked harder, few who have had less regard to results, than I. No false shame shall prevent my saying this — when I feel like it. Now if I could go to sleep for five years, I think I should be rested."

— *WGE to JFC, January 28, 1846*

* * *

"In St. Louis at the end of three years I could not calculate upon an audience of more than 25 or 30, in pleasant weather."

— *WGE, Notebook entry, 1847*

* * *

"The annoyance of visitors is awful. Two hours, today, exclusively a bore. Yet I cannot avoid it, without loss of more, on the whole, than I can gain.

"Another hour in the same way so that except hearing the lessons of my two scholars I have done nothing today and (it is now after 12:30 A.M.) and what is worse, I am tired. A specimen of too many days."

— *WGE, Notebook entry, June, 1848*

* * *

CHAPTER II
"THE WHOLE CITY WAS HIS PARISH" (1849)

"This year everything sad is heaped upon us."

"If I use the next year rightly it will be the best and richest of my life." So wrote William Greenleaf Eliot in his journal on the day after Christmas, 1848. It was not unusual, at the turning of the year, or sometimes in the fall, for Eliot to record in his journal his thoughts, plans or ideas for the year ahead. These jottings not only give us the specifics of his objectives and goals; they also reveal a characteristically optimistic and hopeful spirit. Only rarely did he turn to reflection about the past; his orientation, and the orientation of the progressive era in which he lived, was towards the future. Typifying this spirit was the sentence with which he concluded an address written late in his life relating the remarkable history of the Church of the Messiah on the occasion of its fiftieth anniversary: "The past has much for which we may reasonably be grateful, but the future must and will have better things in store."

But more than just an optimistic, forward-looking spirit supported Eliot's prophecy of December 26, 1848. 1849 would mark the fifteenth anniversary of his arrival in St. Louis. In that time the population of the city had increased ten-fold, from barely 7000 to over 70,000. By following a maxim other young clergymen would do well to emulate, not to use their influence until they have some, he was gradually emerging as one of the leading citizens of this rapidly-growing city and would eventually become generally considered its most influential minister. His church, likewise growing in numbers and influence, had already really outgrown its original building at Fourth and Pine which they had built in 1837, even with a major addition in 1842 which had increased the seating capacity of the church by fully a half. One of Eliot's plans for the year ahead was the construction of a new church, a project that was fully launched by year's end despite the then-unforseen calamities of the months ahead.

"My time is all broken in little pieces," Eliot wrote in his journal, a not uncommon ministerial lament. Though his activities and involvements outside the church were at this time miniscule compared to what they would become in later years, even at this point he was deeply concerned that "secular" activities occupied too much of his attention and energy, distracting him from his first purposes. Sunday newspapers were introduced in St. Louis around this time. Eliot declined to subscribe, however, because he said he felt it tended to "secularize" the day too much. Sundays, at least, he reserved for God. His journal meditation on the day after Christmas in 1848 reveals his state of mind as he looked ahead:

What I must do in the coming year:

Regularly have an hour, if I can, at least half an hour, in my study, before breakfast: For personal religious improvement.

Sermons. Since I began to preach, I have never preached *one* that satisfied me, and generally the hour after preaching is one of commingled pain and mortification. Yet I fear there is more of *self* than of true humility in this. Let me *try harder and fret less.*

If I use the next year rightly it will be the best and richest of my life. I must now use, for more extended good, the influence which I feel myself to have acquired. As a *Citizen,* I must make myself known, through the state. But still more, in my society, a deeper religious influence must be expected — and this charity begins at home. There are causes that have turned me away from God and from Church, which have now ceased and must cease altogether. . . . If I know myself my first object in life is to make my own people religious — but the details of life, public schools, etc. engross too much time.

When Eliot first became a member of the St. Louis School Board in 1848 the public schools were at a primitive level. He spent some time visiting the various schools and, having found them generally substandard, he instigated the "importation" of a number of new teachers from New England. (Four of them lodged initially in the Eliots' home.)

Besides his considerable work as a member of the School Board and continuing pastoral duties, Eliot was also appointed at this time a member of a commission to investigate conditions at the county farm and city workhouse and to initiate a proposal for a new correctional facility. "Those who are able to work all the time without painful weariness," he confided to his journal, "do not know what luxury they enjoy."

Nevertheless, his plans around this time, besides those already mentioned, included a plan to preach on slavery; to approach members of the legislature regarding some consideration of emancipation laws; to preach strongly against the liquor trade; to deliver a series of lectures on his European travels of the year before, for the benefit of the church's charity fund; and to give a course of religious lectures for young men and women. Such were some of the "little pieces" of his life.

But a major focus of his energies was the public schools, and particularly on his own idea to get passed in the state legislature an authorization for a city property tax — an authorization for a tax not exceeding one-tenth of one percent — and its approval by the voters of the city. The enabling legislation was approved by the State General Assembly on February 13, 1849 and would be submitted to the voters of St. Louis in June.

Eliot had been elected President of the School Board in October of 1848. This may be seen as a symbol of his increasing influence and at least one basis for his confident expectation of "the best and richest" year of his life in 1849.

But what would prove to be a truer harbinger of the new year was Eliot's journal entry of January 21: "Tomorrow from the church will be buried James Henderson Haven, the first victim of the cholera from my society." In the weeks and months that followed sickness and death were the constant companion and preoccupation not only of the minister and the doctor, but of all the citizens of St. Louis, as a cholera epidemic swept the city which killed more than 10% of the city's population before it abated in late summer. Eliot's journal for these months is an

36

Abby Adams Cranch Eliot
(Mrs. William Greenleaf Eliot)
(Courtesy Washington University Archives)

almost constant record of death-bed visitation and funerals, interspersed with School Board meetings — support was needed for the school tax vote in June — and of course the unbroken routine of preaching and worship.

"Things are very gloomy and becoming worse," he wrote during this period, "but one subject engrosses all minds. In one family five persons have died since Wednesday, and like cases I hear of daily." Both days and nights were filled with calls to the dying. Week by week the number of deaths increased. On a Tuesday during this period he recorded for himself a "comparatively quiet day," yet the previous morning he had gone twice to visit an Edward Crow, who died at one o'clock. At seven in the evening he christened a baby whose mother had died, and then at eight o'clock went to a School Board meeting. At half past nine he received a message from a Mrs. Gates, whose husband he had previously visited. He found her alone with Dr. Gates, who was not expected to live through the night. The neighbors were all sick, and he persuaded the tired wife to sleep, while he remained during the night with the sick man. These people lived in a small, one-story brick house, on low ground, with a bed on the floor. With careful nursing Dr. Gates got through the night very well, and when Eliot left him there was some hope of his recovery. He returned to his home in the morning and, sending a physician to the sick man he had just left, went to bed and slept three hours, when he was summoned to a Mrs. Holden and her child, both ill. At three in the afternoon she sent for him a second time, and as soon as he saw her he "knew that she must die." He spent most of the afternoon with her and returned in the evening after attending a wedding. At midnight he was again summoned to her bedside and remained there until three in the morning. On coming home he met at his door a gentleman who told him that his "next neighbor," Mrs. Clark, was very ill. At seven thirty the previous evening she had been at Eliot's door. He had discouraged her from returning to nurse a cholera patient. At nine o'clock she was violently ill, and at four-thirty in the morning, when he reached her bedside, she was in a dying condition.

And so the record continues.

As if the cholera were not enough, on the evening of May 17, a fire broke out on the 262-ton steamer White Cloud which was tied up on the riverfront at the foot of Franklin Street. Fanned by a strong northeast wind, the blaze quickly spread to other boats along the river and in about half an hour 23 steamers, three barges and one canal boat were destroyed. Embers carried across the levee to the wood frame buildings that began at Locust and Front Streets, and before the fire was brought under control (by the drastic measure of blowing up a line of buildings along Second and Market Streets) 400 buildings were damaged or destroyed along 15 city blocks. The total loss was estimated at 6.5 million dollars.

In June Eliot wrote in his journal: "This year everything sad is heaped upon us."

Besides the personal tragedy which the epidemic and the fire entailed, they also seemed to insure the defeat of the school tax measure. Even the normally sanguine Eliot confided to his journal, "I fear that all hope of a tax for the schools is lost by this fire." But he was wrong.

In later years Eliot credited the successful passage of the tax largely to members of his congregation who went door to door canvassing voters. Eliot always referred to the fact that the vote was two to one in favor, and this is the statistic that is usually reported. It ought to be noted, however, that in a city with a population of about 70,000 there were only six thousand voters in 1849, and of these barely more than 700 voted on the school tax measure at all. But the measure was won, and Eliot recorded his satisfaction:

. . . now that the law is *passed* and *confirmed,* I feel as if this alone is a good and sufficient year's work. It is enough in itself to make me satisfied that I returned to St. Louis.

Eliot once said that the passage of the school tax marked the true beginning of the St. Louis public schools. Typical of the Unitarians of the period, Eliot felt that education was the primary and best means for the improvement of society. A school for the poor was one of the earliest charities of the Church. And the importance of the St. Louis public schools on the future course of history was a theme in Eliot's Phi Beta Kappa Address, delivered near the end of the Civil War:

> The newspaper correspondent may tell you that Missouri was saved to the Union by the taking of Camp Jackson and the scattering of the disloyal legislature three days before an ordinance of secession would have been passed. But the earnest of that victory had been given twenty-five years before by the establishment in St. Louis of the New England system of free education. On the first Monday of June, 1849, when fully one half the city had just been destroyed by fire, the citizens determined, by a vote of two to one, to tax themselves for the support of the public schools. On that day the victory was gained.

There may be more faith than fact in this assertion, but for the St. Louis of 1849 the secure financing of its school system, which became one of the finest in the country, was unquestionably a great step forward, even though it seems doubtful that Eliot — or anyone at the time — would have made a connection between its accomplishment and the looming conflict which would in a few years shatter the nation. Civil war was then no more than a storm cloud on the distant horizon. Slavery, on the other hand, was an ever-present reality.

Given Eliot's evident and unequivocal abhorrence of slavery, his apparent patience with it may be very difficult for us to understand today, removed in time, even as it was misunderstood by many in his own day, who were however removed in space from direct association with the society in which slavery was a common, deeply-rooted part. Eliot's willingness to move slowly on the eradication of slavery, which he considered an absolute evil, is a social expression of what I have termed his conservative radicalism. He suffered harsh censure from Northern ministers who found even his continuing residence in a slave state to be highly questionable. He was accused of secret sympathies toward slavery, even of being a slave-holder himself. He once referred to an "eminent preacher in an Eastern city" who had said of him by way of rebuke that "for a Unitarian clergyman to preach in such a manner as to be endured in a slave state was good evidence of his unfaithfulness." Slavery, and its attendant evils, was a fact of everyday life in the St. Louis of the 1840s, one no citizen and certainly no minister could escape.

In his one real book, a biography of a former slave named Archer Alexander, whom he helped to free, Eliot wrote, "Notwithstanding the comparative humanity of slavery as an institution in Missouri, I can truthfully say that there is nothing in all the scenes of *Uncle Tom's Cabin,* as given by Mrs. Stowe, to which I cannot find a parallel in what I have myself seen and known in St. Louis."

As an example, he described a scene that occurred when he was living on Market Street, near Third. He was in his study, overlooking the yard of a neighbor, when

> I was startled by a terrible scream, and, going to the window, saw under an open shed a young mulatto woman tied up to the joist by her thumbs, so that her feet scarcely touched the ground, stripped from her shoulders to her hips, and a man standing by her with cowhide whips in hand. He had paused for a moment from his scourging to see if she would "give in." I opened the window to call out to him. He told me to "shut up and mind my own business." But he feared publicity just enough to untie the victim and stop his brutality for a time.

Eliot went straight to the grand jury, then in session, and entered a complaint. As a result the man was brought before the criminal court (then being held in the basement of the Unitarian Church while the Court House was undergoing repair. "Those were primitive days in St. Louis," Eliot notes.). Eliot witnessed, and the case was fully proved. The offense of the colored girl was her unwillingness to submit to the wishes of her master. Nonetheless, the verdict was not guilty, "because as afterwards declared, the penalty fixed by law was thought to be too severe."

"Attempt was also made to invalidate my testimony as that of a sentimental young preacher who knew nothing of slavery. That was a strong point to make," Eliot added ironically. This kind of thing, though as he says not typical, was nonetheless part of the reality with which he lived.

An early entry in the first volume of his journal reflects Eliot's deep revulsion against the "peculiar institution":

> I have been in St. Louis fourteen years, in which time no one subject has been so often in my mind as slavery. Upon no other have I been more anxious to do what is right. My detestation of the system is very great, my sense of wrong to the black and the injury to the white very deep. I never pass by the slave jails on Olive Street without saying almost, sometimes quite loud: "May the curse of God abide on this vile traffic!" Yet I have spoken of it in public comparatively seldom, only once or twice each year. In conversation I have always spoken freely. Has it been through want of moral courage? I think not. Certainly not through self-seeking. I have had everything to gain and nothing to lose. Ten years ago I had only to come out as an "abolitionist," and although I would have been required to leave my place here, I could have returned to friends and kindred with the honor of a martyr, without his losses; covered with glory; and with the certainty of good settlement. But my gain would have been the only gain.
>
> I have waited; in patience possessing my soul; perhaps I must wait a little longer — not much. The influence I have now acquired is real; by proper and fearless exertions it will become deeper and wider.

Actually, by the time he wrote this he had already sought to use the influence of his pen as well as his voice in behalf of gradual emancipation, his preferred course for the eradication of slavery over a period of years. Using various *noms de plume* he had argued this position in letters published in the public press. (He signed some of these letters ERGON, but abandoned it when he realized it was an anagram of Negro.) And in January of 1849 he wrote long letters to William Campbell in the Missouri Senate and to United States Senator Thomas H. Benton, discussing the slavery issue in considerable detail and urging legislation mandating gradual emancipation:

> A residence of more than fourteen years in St. Louis and careful observation of the progress of society, not only in the city, but throughout the State, have led me to believe that the institution of slavery is the greatest obstacle, perhaps the only obstacle, by which our moral, social and general advance as a people is hindered.
>
> Next to the immediate duties of my profession, therefore, there is no object which I have so much at heart as the commencement of some movement by which an emancipation law in some form or other could be secured. . . . I believe that the public mind is so far prepared that if you were to take the lead, the majority are ready to follow. If you will consent to draw up a law providing for the gradual emancipation of our slaves, say in a course of ten, twenty, or thirty years, upon some system which would protect the interests of all parties as far as possible, it would become the law of the land before three years had passed. . . . My own feelings are in favor of prudent, conservative legislation, and I believe that all great changes in the social system, to be well made, must be gradual. But the beginning cannot be made too soon. . . .

These letters help us to understand Eliot's position as a gradual emancipationist, but they inspired no action on the part of the legislators, though Benton, at least, was certainly sympathetic. Eliot's influence outside of St. Louis was still slight, and in this instance he seems to have misread the state of the public mind in Missouri. Benton, whose personal popularity and influence were great, was defeated for re-election to the Senate the following year, largely because of his anti-slavery views.

Eliot said repeatedly in later years that his preaching with regard to slavery had had only one theme, "do as you would be done by." He believed that real reform occurs only in the hearts and minds of individuals. And he had what many may regard as a naive faith in both the power of the gospel and the power of the good.

In February Eliot preached a sermon taking as his text Jesus' parable of the mustard seed, the tiny grain which becomes a great tree. Based on the notes that survive, in this sermon Eliot argued that Christ proposed a radical change in society, but that he did not expect it to be a rapid change. Thus he had given his injunctions to individuals who are the seeds of the great tree of righteousness. "Blessed are the peacemakers," Jesus had said, because wars begin in the human heart, and it is our hearts which must be overcome if wars are to cease.

> The primary object of Christianity is not to change the external features of society, but to regenerate the individual soul, which must be done, not by direct acts of superior power, but in accordance with the law of voluntary action. . . . One must labor for social reform, by moral means, by individual reform. Mere changes of institutions will do little good.

Here Eliot was dealing with the perennial issue of the relationship of means and ends. Not only cannot good ends be achieved by evil means, but true and permanent changes were less likely to be achieved by coercive power than by voluntary action. "Sudden changes of institutions," he argued, were "never as good as gradual changes." As examples, he drew from both ancient and modern history, citing the Israelites forty years in the wilderness, the history of Europe, especially in the period of the Reformation, and a comparison of the French Revolution with that of England in the 1680s.

This background provided the theoretical framework for his explanation of why he favored gradual emancipation rather than immediate abolition. The evil of slavery, he said, was absolute. No one saw this more clearly than he. It was an "unqualified curse," and "individually we sin to countenance or extend it." But even so, it must be borne in mind that "a great change, even from bad to good, *takes time*." However, far from counseling mere patience, an indefinite continuation of the *status quo*, this very fact made it, he said, "even more important to *begin* at once." There were two main ways of working towards this end. One was through voluntary associations. But in this sermon he stressed the second, the necessity of individual action.

Whether, if the course of action urged by Eliot and the other gradual emancipationists had been followed, the Civil War could have been averted is of course a matter of continuing historical speculation. However deeply felt and sincerely expressed, Eliot's faith in the power of the gospel over individual hearts and minds, and of the gradual but sure attainment of good over evil appeared to many in his own time — even as it does to many today — merely a rationalization for cowardice, conservatism, or even, as we have mentioned, secret pro-slavery sentiments, all accusations actually hurled against him. One thing is clear. Eliot had a deep understanding of slavery and the society of which it was a part. He knew it not just as abstract evil, but as a heinous personal and social reality, deeply ingrained in the social and economic structures of the South. No one understood better than he the degree of personal and social disruption its eradication would entail.

And whether naive or not, Eliot's faith in the efficacy of gospel influence rather than political coercion was justified in his own experience among his own

41

people. By 1856, he later reported, "not one of our regular supporters held a slave in bondage, except in two or three instances where emancipation would have been cruelty."

It seems likely, however, that this accomplishment could not be entirely attributed to changes of moral perspective among all the former slaveholders in the constituency of the Church of the Messiah. Some no doubt kept their slaves and left the church.

But overall the congregation continued to grow. Whatever losses there may have been as the church entered into the increasingly divisive years preceding the Civil War, they were insufficient even to delay plans to begin construction of a new (and expensive) church building. By the end of 1849 Eliot had already picked out the location, the northwest corner of Ninth and Olive, and was urging the project forward. The building, a magnificent edifice designed to seat 1200 or more in the pews, would be considered the most beautiful church in the city, and would be filled to overflowing on the day of its formal dedication two years later, on November 7, 1851.

In Chapter I, we recounted Eliot's refusal, in 1847, of the position of General Secretary of the American Unitarian Association, and speculated that in returning to St. Louis he had a most compelling need to justify his life (and therefore his decision to return) by great and good accomplishment. Both church and community benefitted from his decision, but it meant that an often weak body labored ever more intensely, and not without consequence.

Letters and the Notebooks during the years 1847 through 1851 are regularly dotted with references to Eliot's physical weakness and disabilities. Twice in these years, with his congregation's support, he went to Europe, partly for health reasons. Between these trips abroad he was urged in a letter from concerned parishioners to cease preaching altogether until his health improved. An Assistant Minister, the Reverend Hassal, was called to the church during this period, not only to fill the pulpit during Eliot's absences but to assist generally in preaching and other pastoral duties. Yet despite ill health, it appears that Eliot worked harder than ever, particularly through St. Louis' year of trial and crisis, 1849.

And by its end, a different kind of man than Eliot might have questioned or reconsidered his decision of barely two years earlier to return to St. Louis rather than accept a position of some importance and prestige in Boston. An amusing incident involving the man who was chosen to fill the position of General Secretary of the American Unitarian Association after Eliot declined it, the Reverend F. W. Holland, occurred just before Christmas at the end of 1849. Holland presented himself at Eliot's house one afternoon and apparently behaved in such a manner that the servants and others thought he was crazy. Matters were straightened out after Eliot returned home, but he noted in his journal that night, "Common sense is a very rare commodity, especially among parsons."

True to his nature, Eliot never looked back. But the year of trial and his increasing debility had their effect. A certain morbidity creeps into Eliot's journal, even as his activity continued unabated. Perhaps in part to justify his decision to return to St. Louis, but also because the exigencies of circumstances required it, Eliot worked even harder than before. He felt the responsibilities of his increasing influence, the rising crisis in public affairs, the continuing demands of preaching and parish work, including now the building and financing of a new large church. School Board responsibilities continued even after the major accomplishment of the tax measure. And on top of all this had come the extremities of the cholera epidemic and the fire. On the last day of July he had counted the number of children for whom he had some measure of responsibility and discovered they numbered 26 — these, of course, beyond his own.

On July 22 he wrote in his journal,

I am inexpressibly shocked today to hear of the death of Rev. Mr. Vancourt. Nothing has brought me so strongly to a sense of the danger to which I have been and am exposed, or of the mercy of God by which I have so far been preserved. He came to see me ten days since, and we talked over our several trials and labors. He has been very faithful as a pastor, and very useful. . . . Yesterday at four P.M. he was apparently well, and died at three this morning. It is a further warning to me, and as far as duty will allow, I shall take it to myself.

As to the theory of contagion: I have tried it, I think, very thoroughly, not only in the ordinary exposure of nursing and doctoring, but sometimes I have held the hand of the suffering, an hour at a time, throughout the whole sickness, conversing with him so feeble that in order to hear the words I have had to lean over and breathe the same breath, even in the last hour of life — and after death, in kneeling near the coffin, have incurred the further risk of post mortem contagion. This over and over again, by night and by day, when tired and unwell myself, but without harm.

Two weeks later he wrote, "When will it all end? I do now so long for freedom from care and anxiety that I am almost sick at heart."

The epidemic abated in late summer, and on September 4, Eliot left St. Louis on what he called an "indefinite excursion." "How far I shall go is uncertain. My mind must have entire relief from ordinary cares in preparation for the winter's campaign." But relief did not mean rest, at least not much. He wrote these words in Tremont, Illinois, where he had "spent four days, preached five times, and on Sunday afternoon organized a church." A few days later he was in Peoria, where he noted that he had made arrangements for the purchase of a lot and the erection of a chapel. He next visited Chicago and met with representatives of the church there which was having financial problems and drew up a proposal for them before leaving for a journey eastward to Buffalo and Boston, where he preached, and then to New Bedford, New York, Philadelphia and finally Washington, where he spent some time at his family's home.

Over the years Eliot frequently emphasized the fact that his only Ordination was as an Evangelist, and he took this charge seriously. He had been Ordained on August 17, 1834, at the Federal Street Church in Boston. William Ellery Channing — the Minister of Federal Street Church who is generally regarded as the founder of American Unitarianism — was in the chancel, although he apparently took no formal part in the Ordination service. (Channing had married Eliot's parents.) James Freeman Clarke preached the sermon, taking as his text John 10:14, and the Ordaining Prayer was given by Henry Ware, Jr. Eliot's Certificate of Ordination stated that he had been "ordained . . . to the work of the Gospel Ministry as an Evangelist, whenever Providence may open to him a field of labor." The call to St. Louis had already been extended at the time, but it became obvious that Eliot considered wherever he happened to be a part of his "field of labor." Evangelism, in both the institutional sense of creating and sustaining new churches and in the personal sense of bringing souls to Christ, was a major focus of Eliot's life.

In 1836, in an article for the *Western Messenger,* he declared simply and boldly:

Every Christian sect ought to have its missionaries, who should be sent to every part of the world where they will be favorably received. Christianity was from the beginning a missionary enterprise, and must remain so until the whole world is Christian.

Noting that Unitarian "missionary efforts" had been very limited, he said that "upon the whole . . . Unitarians are not much to blame for their past inaction [due to limited resources and other factors, but] are to blame for their present inaction."

43

At times it seems as if Eliot was determined to make up for this lack all by himself. And the year 1849 concluded with several weeks of missionary work, piled upon the months of almost ceaseless pastoral and other labor in St. Louis. The physical, mental and emotional exertions of the year had at least one dramatic physical consequence.

Early in 1850, the graceful and beautiful writing in Eliot's journal is suddenly replaced by an equally legible, but somewhat uncertain, handwriting, slanted to the left instead of to the right. It begins, "By some singular affliction which is a sort of paralysis of the muscles of the right arm, I am losing the faculty of writing." So for more than two years Eliot wrote exclusively with his left hand. As always, he looked to the future, but now with a sense of foreboding: "Perhaps it is only a first indication that a constitution, naturally feeble, is about to give way."

MISCELLANY, 1850–1852

"I have always thought that you and I were created as psychological complements in friendship, and some day propose to 'carry out' the idea to our mutual satisfaction; but not now. They used to sing a refrain to an anti-VanBuren song, "Van, Van is a used up man;" and I can scarcely refrain from using it daily of myself. I am used up almost beyond patching; and am now considering whether it is worth while to try a patching process once more, by [travelling] 8 or 10 months, or not. I will advise you of the result.

"My wife is a jewel. My children are five in number and well in health. My head aches and I am sick at the stomach and sleepy.

"But I am tenderly attached to you, have the highest esteem for your wife and would be tenderly attached to her if I dared, love your children because they are yours. . . ."

— WGE to James Freeman Clarke, October 17, 1850

*　　　*　　　*

"Resolved, That the Trustees of the First Congregational Society fully concur with their Pastor Rev. Mr. Eliot in the necessity and propriety of his having some relaxation from his pastoral duties, and they cheerfully acquiesce in his proposal to be absent for 10 or 12 months, believing it will contribute to the restoration of his health. They therefore urge him to go and beg to assure him that he carries with him their earnest wishes and prayers for the health and happiness of himself and his family, and a sincere hope he may return to the sphere of his usefulness with re-established health, where he will be heartily welcomed by his parishioners."

— from the Records of the Church of the Messiah
(First Congregational Society of St. Louis)
November 11, 1850

*　　　*　　　*

"Mr. Eliot had just commenced his sermon when fire was discovered in the back part of the building. At the first alarm there was a rush to get out of the church. Mr. Eliot spoke to them saying there was no danger. Some went out and some stayed. Mr. Eliot did not finish his sermon, said the minds of the people were too much excited. The furnace it seems was injured by the workmen and set fire to some of the wood work. It was soon put out and little harm done."

— Diary of Sarah Smith (Flagg), December 14, 1851

*   *   *

On February 9, 1852, James Freeman Clarke signed a letter to Eliot: "Yours, with wonderful love — (passing that of women)." Eliot of course recognized the Biblical reference. In his reply on March 2, he referred to Clarke's closing and commented: "In the time of Jonathan and David, before women's rights were discovered, that may have been correct, but at present my wife demurs."

*   *   *

"Am elected President of the Institute for the Blind, in place of Dr. Potts who died two weeks ago."

— WGE, Notebook entry, April 14, 1852

*   *   *

"Called at Knoff's book bindery, and found them just beginning to letter back of my books Doctrinal Sermons; William G. *Elliot*, Jr. — just in time to correct it at expense of making a new die."

— WGE, Notebook entry, April 14, 1852

*   *   *

"I have just bought a horse and carriage — $400. Which is almost wrong; but for sake of own health and that of family may be pardonable."

— WGE, Notebook entry, May 1852

*   *   *

William Greenleaf Eliot circa 1854
(Courtesy Washington University Archives)

CHAPTER III
ELIOT SEMINARY (1857)

"An 'Eliot Seminary' has been incorporated by [the] present legislature but I know nothing of it."

(WGE Notebook entry, February 22, 1853)

On Christmas Day, 1852, Ralph Waldo Emerson arrived in St. Louis to deliver a series of seven lectures. Eliot's journal is silent on Emerson's visit, but in a letter back to Concord, Emerson commented on the "sumptuous church" — he meant the new Church of the Messiah, then only a year old — and its minister's "really good sermons." "Mr. Eliot," wrote Emerson, "is the Saint of the West."

The Saint of the West was 41 years old. The population of St. Louis was over 80,000, with more people arriving every day. Eliot was the pastor of a large and flourishing church whose membership and constituency included some of St. Louis' most prominent and influential citizens, now proudly housed in what was generally considered its most beautiful church building.

Sarah Smith, a young member of the congregation who served at times as Eliot's amanuensis, wrote in her diary on September 7, 1851, that the new church building was opened for inspection for the first time on that day:

> As a whole I like it, but there are some things I don't like. The angels have very old faces and are supporting columns which the ceiling rests on — the poor little old things look as if they would be crushed by the weight of them. . . . It is very neat and elegant, but it makes little difference, I know, about these things. We do not go to worship the church but the God who dwells there.

The building was Dedicated as the Church of the Messiah on Sunday morning, December 7, 1851. Designed to accommodate 1200 people in the pews, Eliot recorded that "not less than 1500" crowded into the Sanctuary for the Dedication Service, which he conducted. Mr. Hassal, the Associate Pastor, read the Scriptures; the Rev. John Heywood of Louisville offered the Prayer of Dedication; the Rev. A. A. Livermore of Cincinnati preached the sermon; and the Rev. Mr. Fuller of the Quincy, Illinois church — one of the many societies Eliot had helped organize on his evangelizing trips — gave the Concluding Prayer. 250 to 300 people gathered that afternoon for the monthly Communion Service, "of whom many were of other churches." And at the evening service Eliot delivered a sermon on the history of the society and its prospects for the future.

Despite the large congregation that had gathered for the Dedication Service, the sale of pews the next day was not a great success. Pew sales were the traditional means of paying for church buildings, and apparently fewer than 40 were sold. Also, the church — which would not be fully completed for another year — was costing more than originally expected. The stained glass windows were damaged in transit from Philadelphia and had to be returned. The main tower was still unfinished. The ultimate cost of the building, including the lot and a magnificent $5000 organ Eliot had purchased in Boston, was in excess of $105,000, as against an early estimate of $40,000. And almost a year after the Dedication, nearly half the total cost was unprovided for.

Eliot later related the circumstances under which the church was fully paid for by the time of its actual completion:

> A meeting of twenty gentlemen was held at the house of John Tilden, October 19, 1852, to devise ways and means. After considering the case as one, first, of honor and honesty, and next of duty in the cause of religious truth and allegiance to Christ, it was resolved then and there to pay the debt and be done with it. By donations varying from $100 to $3000, *several persons borrowing the money they gave,* and by the disposal of pews, the whole amount was raised, so that every obligation was met. [Italics added.]

Both the approach and the result were typical, including the willingness of some to incur personal debt so that the church would be free and clear. In another place Eliot noted that because of this commitment the church was out of debt, but that those involved would "ever know the amount of personal sacrifice involved in the accomplishment of the desired result."

It was far from the last time that the people of the Church of the Messiah would be called upon for money. But of the hundreds of thousands of dollars they would give in response to their pastor's appeals in the ensuing years, only the barest fraction would go to the relatively slight operating costs of the church itself and none at all to the building of a church endowment. The money which might have become the endowment fund of the Church of the Messiah was directed instead to creating and sustaining institutions in the community, and one in particular above all.

On February 22, 1853, Eliot made what has become perhaps the most famous notation in his journal: "An 'Eliot Seminary' has been incorporated by [the] present legislature; but I know nothing of it." It was on this date that Governor Sterling Price signed into law a bill sponsored by Wayman Crow, drygoods wholesaler, State Senator and a member of the Church of the Messiah — a charter for an educational institution. The story, factual even though it has taken on some of the character of myth, has been many times told.

Crow, in his second term in the State Legislature, happened to see on a colleague's desk a model charter which struck him, he said, as "particularly good." Using it, and without consulting anyone, he drew up a charter for a tax-free educational institution in the City of St. Louis to be called Eliot Seminary, and named himself, William Greenleaf Eliot, and 15 other members of the Church of the Messiah as incorporators. Thus was Washington University conceived, though its actual birth would have to be placed at some point in the future. There were perhaps no more than the usual labor pains, but it seemed for awhile as if the child would never be named.

Writing of Crow's independent action, Eliot later wrote:

> It took us by surprise, and, at first thought, caused some amusement; for none of us had dreamed of such a thing, and an educational enterprise seemed quite

beyond our strength. But, upon examination of the charter, it was found to be a document of extraordinary merit, and capable of grandest use. Its possession constituted a divine call; and, after talking it over for a year, we determined to organize under it, and go to work.

Thus it was almost a year later, on February 13, 1854, that the incorporators met formally for the first time. They elected Eliot President of the Board, determined to seek funds to launch an industrial school and college, and heard Eliot's objection to the name "Eliot Seminary" as being both too personal and too ecclesiastical.

George Washington was in 1854 still the one true national hero, and he was a special hero of Eliot's. This, and the coincidental date of the signing of the Charter on February 22, no doubt suggested the adoption of the name Washington Institute. They used the name informally for a year or so before someone worried about the legalities, and Mr. Crow was asked to introduce an amendment to the Charter in the State Legislature. Before he could do so, however, a bill introduced by a Senator Holmes chartering another school, Washington College in St. Louis, was passed and signed into law.

Whatever the intentions of the incorporators of the Washington College, a mainly Presbyterian group, there would be obvious confusion to have two schools called Washington in St. Louis, so some "unauthorized parties" (according to the University corporate records) introduced an amendment to change the name of the Unitarian's effort to "Lafayette Institute" instead of Washington. This bill was actually passed in the Missouri Legislature and on the desk of the governor when he received a telegraphic message from St. Louis asking him to veto it.

Eliot noted in his journal in late summer or early fall of 1854:

I am engaged in beginning foundation for an Educational Institute under charter of 'Eliot Seminary': to consist of male and female and Industrial departments. It will require large endowment.

Col. O'Fallon has promised two Blocks of ground near the Reservoir for Industrial School; the present value is $25,000 or more.

This was the first such gift received, and in the later complications regarding the name, it was proposed to name the school the O'Fallon Institute. Colonel O'Fallon gave his consent, and the board voted to accept the new name. But it was then announced that the Washington College group had abandoned their project and upon learning this O'Fallon withdrew consent to use his name.

It was another two years before the charter was actually amended, with one other change, so that in 1857 "Eliot Seminary" became officially "Washington University."

But for the first thirty years of its existence, Washington University was in every respect except its name Eliot University. And in some ways it seems unfortunate that the University has not actually taken this name to honor the particular contribution of the man whose vision and effort laid the foundation for all that was to follow.

The name Washington symbolized Eliot's vision for the fledgling school; he envisioned a truly national university in a St. Louis which would be the central city of the great new American republic growing in the west. In his view Washington University would be a primary spiritual resource shedding its influence throughout the land, even as St. Louis was the center through which the natural resources of the prairie would flow to feed the nation. This may seem grandiose, so baldly stated, but it was the era of grandiosity, and a progressive spirit. St. Louis at this time was truly the gateway to the west, a west which represented the new and untried, unlimited horizons. Eliot was not troubled by these characteristics; in fact, in important respects he embodied them. But he was gravely concerned that traditional standards of morality and virtue would be lost in the social disruption created by rapid progress. Eliot was a latter-day Puritan in a new New World.

To the Puritan, the only really important progress was spiritual progress. But this did not imply a preoccupation with other-worldly concerns. Service to humanity was part of one's duty to God and was to be evaluated in those terms. Eliot saw the University as a spiritual enterprise whose benefits would be not only immediate and narrow, limited to scholars or a single community, but broad and long-ranging, lifting the character of a whole region and benefiting ultimately the nation as a whole. But even beyond that, Eliot possessed and communicated a sincere belief that he was engaged not just in man's good works but in God's high purposes. This was no doubt a source of his influence over others.

At the second meeting of the Incorporators of Eliot Seminary, on February 22, 1854, a year after the original charter had been granted, Eliot addressed the group formally as to the specific goals and objectives of their endeavor. After discussing in some detail the nature of the school he envisioned, he said,

> We propose an Institution for the public benefit. This, perhaps considered on a large scale, is the strongest motive by which we are actuated. We live in that part of the United States which will probably give character to the whole country in future generations. Our city will, probably, be one of the largest and most influential in the Western Valley. The necessity of laying a broad and substantial foundation for educational, religious and philanthropic institutions, is, therefore, strong and imperative. . . .
>
> Our feelings and our sense of duty, therefore [lead us] to invest a generous part of that which by honest industry we have earned for the public benefit. We desire to leave the city in every way better than we found it.

In this way Eliot broached the subject of financial support to the Trustees. He knew that noble sentiments would not create the school he envisioned, but he cast his appeals for money in the highest terms of duty and public service.

Eliot understood money. One commentator wrote: "No man of the cloth seems to have been more practical about money than Mr. Eliot, nor more able to inspire other men to be impractical."

In 1864, ten years after his initial address to the Trustees, he was able to report that $478,000 had been contributed to Washington University, four-fifths of which had come from members of his church. Eliot himself made a not unsubstantial contribution, reaped not from his salary, but from his continuous investment in small amounts of land in the rapidly expanding city. A St. Louis businessman was once prompted to remark that if he could have had Mr. Eliot for his partner together they would have made most of the money west of the Alleghenies.

So Eliot understood money, the benefits it could bring, but he also understood the threat which the pursuit of wealth represented to the values he held to be supreme:

> [The] Principal motive to come west is that of making money. . . . [T]his universal is the greatest danger to the ultimate prosperity of St. Louis. . . . [I] fear that religion and morality and education and everything which makes people truly prosperous will bow down to one God, mammon. . . .
>
> They who value literature and religion, and feel the importance of education and morality, must come forward and establish institutions by which public opinion may be elevated, public feeling and taste purified, and the community saved from forgetting that there is something real in the world besides money; that there are purely intellectual pleasures which money cannot buy, and intellectual and moral wants that money cannot satisfy. . . .

Eliot's great gift was to be able to obtain money and employ it effectively toward the higher and nobler purposes of life, and Washington University was to be the most spectacular example of this capacity.

But not the only one. In the spring of 1856 he replied to a letter from Professor Frederic Huidekoper requesting funds for the support of the Meadville Theological School, a new Unitarian seminary in Pennsylvania, by enumerating the various missions his church was already supporting:

> I do not like to fail in meeting so munificent a proposition and on the other fear to name a new project to my people! Last year $3000 for Alton; this year $2000 for Keokuk; Peoria has sounded a preparatory trumpet; and when your letter was received an agent from Jacksonville was in my room explaining to a committee the necessity of at least $5000 there, from us, to aid in Evangelizing the 1500 students and scholars in that town! Our Ministry-at-Large costs $3000 per annum. To [the Western] Conference $700. . . . To our [Eliot] Seminary and [Washington] Institute for the years '54, '55, '56 over $50,000 and at least $20,000 more must come, if I can possibly get it.

The work of the church and its broadening demands on its pastor continued even as the University became a major focus of attention. Eliot preached twice each Sunday, morning and evening, and conducted a third service with Communion on the first Sunday of each month. Before church he conducted a Sunday School class. A mid-week service was held on Wednesday evening, and Eliot sometimes gave lecture series on other weekday evenings. He repeated sermons, of course, and preached more or less extemporaneously on occasion, but the continuing demand on time and energy were great.

His concern with better organizing his time led him to outline a schedule of his weekly routine; beside a chart he made some notes on his proposed personal schedule:

"To rise, say at 7 or 7:30 as the season advances; which is as early as I can count upon — after Family Prayer, breakfast at 7:30 or 8."

He reserved mornings and early afternoons for sermon writing, study and preparation "for whatever comes next."

Afternoons from 2:30 or 3 to 6 were reserved for "visiting and pastoral cares: . . . my strength is not equal to more than 3 hours of walking or visiting each day. This arrangement for [the afternoon] is for every day in the week, but Sunday."

Finally, evenings he reserved for "Reading, Receiving friends, Religious and other meetings, Letter writing, etc. not to continue, except in extreme cases, later than 12."

Somehow he also found time to continue the evangelizing of the west. As indicated in his letter to Huidekoper, the Church of the Messiah was supporting new churches over a wide geographical area. Early in the summer of 1856 Eliot journeyed for the first time to Milwaukee and pledged $500 toward a subscription to found the "Church of the Redeemer," a church still in existence and now known as the First Unitarian Church.

In September of 1856, Eliot listed in his journal his four major priorities for what he termed "the fall campaign." First came care of the church; second, the Ministry to the poor. The University was third on his list, which he noted was "a heavy care, for an immense amount of money is needed and everything depends upon my exertions. This year ought to find at least $50,000 of Endowment, and I mean that it shall." Last on his list of priorities: "The foundation of a Second Society and church must be laid, and, at least, a lot of ground secured."

The last effort failed. It was not until 1868 that a second Unitarian congregation, the Church of the Unity, was launched and called its first minister, John Calvin Learned. A church building on the north side of Lafayette Square was Dedicated in 1870, a building that still stands, though the Unitarian congregation moved from it in 1915 and moved to a new site on Waterman Boulevard near Kingshighway.

It is possible that a second Unitarian church might have been successfully launched earlier, according to Eliot's intention, had his time and energy not been expended so substantially on University affairs. His journal record is relatively scant during the formative years, but the record of accomplishment is significant.

The first division of the University, the O'Fallon Evening School was opened in October of 1854, and a boys' school, later known as Smith Academy, opened the same year. The Academic Department — which today is called the College — held its first classes in the fall of 1856. The formal Inauguration of Washington University took place on April 23, 1857, with ceremonies featuring an oration delivered that evening at the Mercantile Library Hall by the noted orator, Edward Everett. Mary Institute, the girls' school, welcomed its first students in September of 1859; and not until after this, in October, was the first Chancellor of the University, Joseph G. Hoyt, installed. Thus, during these five formative years, Eliot held functionally the two positions which he would hold formally during the last 17 years of his life, of both Chancellor and President of the Board. The plan of organization of the school and the implementation of this plan were almost entirely in his hands.

Preoccupied as he was with the practical concerns of this enterprise, from the hiring of faculty and furnishing of laboratories to the relentless search for contributions to the endowment of the young institution, Eliot seems never to have lost sight of the broader or spiritual dimensions of his work. In this regard nothing was more important to him, nor more precious to the heritage of the University, than the principle of non-secretarianism embodied in Article VIII of the school's Charter, an article to which Eliot made frequent and pointed reference:

> No instruction, either secretarian in religion, or partisan in politics, shall be allowed in any department of the institution, and no sectarian or partisan test shall be used in the election of professors, teachers, or other officers of the Institute, nor shall any such test ever be used in said Institute for any purpose whatsoever. This article shall be understood as the fundamental condition on which all endowments, of whatever kind, are received.

Eliot told the original University Trustees, all members of his own church it will be recalled:

> [I]t must be our constant endeavor to keep narrow and sectarian influences from every department of the Institute. . . . We believe that the Church and Sunday School, under parental guidance, are the best instructors in religion, and to them the religious training of the young must be chiefly entrusted. The School-room and College are built for a different purpose and have a different work to do.

Notwithstanding this emphasis, the financial support of the University came almost entirely from Unitarians in those early years. The establishment of educational institutions was a relatively common undertaking of churches or denominations in this era, and no doubt many looked upon Washington University, whatever its charter or officers might declare, as a "Unitarian school." Eliot's early efforts to bring non-Unitarians on the Board met with failure, probably for parallel reasons.

In the midst of these labors Eliot suffered what seems to be the greatest personal loss of his lifetime. On January 16, 1855, his beloved first-born child, Mary, died at age 16. Later in the year Eliot edited a series of sermons for publication in a book he entitled *The Discipline of Sorrow.* Though, typically, containing no direct personal references, the motivation for this work was his grief over Mary's death and a desire to offer a source of spiritual comfort to others in like circumstances.

Though the Eliots had by 1855 lost two infant children, Mary's death was something different. The cause of death remains in doubt, but it was apparently a very severe, acute and brief illness. Two days before she died Eliot mentioned in a letter that she was very sick, but there is no indication that he thought even then that she was mortally ill.

Eliot stayed behind when his family went east for the summer of 1855, and on June 10 he wrote to his wife, reflecting upon the death of the daughter who apparently had the nickname or pet name, Molly:

> I do not feel at all *lonely*, though heavy-hearted I must be, for a good while yet. . . . Not that I have either time or disposition to brood over the past. . . . But no one can tell how much I have lost or how constantly it is present with me. I do not mean to complain, and I do not. I can even see why the Chastisement was laid upon me. Nor do I undervalue those precious children that are left to us: But you know how it is. All others cannot take her place, and we must mourn her loss. Dear Molly: daughter and pupil and friend! Well, we have the comfort of knowing that her life was all happy, without cloud to shadow it, from first to last. I think we did our part rightly towards her, and must go on now doing rightly toward the rest.

We have made frequent reference to Eliot's aversion to personal publicity. He himself would never have made the proposal which gave the name to the Women's Department of Washington University. It was launched with a gift of $4000 from four of the Directors of Washington University, subject to two conditions: first, that the school be named Mary Institute; second, that it be chartered on May 11, 1859, which would have been Mary Eliot's twenty-first birthday. Under the circumstances Eliot had no choice but to accept the proposal, though his handwritten notation suggests that he might have thought later to change it: "The name of the Institution was chosen by the Directors of Washington University for the time being, in affectionate memory of Mary Rhodes Eliot."

But beyond personal tragedies and in addition to University activities, pastoral duties and what Eliot called "the nameless but many cares and occupations that break up the time and disturb the thoughts," there was also a nation coming rapidly in these years to a great crisis. St. Louis was in many respects a microcosm of the nation as a whole. It was in a slave-holding state but populated by many whose sympathies lay with the North. In brief, all that divided the nation divided St. Louis; and all that divided St. Louis divided the congregation of the Church of the Messiah. Eliot told a Boston audience after the war that his congregation "had been composed of diverse materials from all parts of the country . . . with all shades of political opinion; with extreme diversity of social prejudices, from the pro-slavery secessionist to the abolitionist of the most ultra school."

In the next chapter we shall see how the Church of the Messiah was affected by and responded to the extremities of Civil War. Before that, it is valuable to have some understanding of Eliot's ideas concerning the relationship of church and society, which is one aspect of his doctrine of the church.

In preparation for a sermon Eliot once defined the "Ecclesiastical Position" of the church of the Messiah under four headings:

First, it was a Christian Church;

Second, it was Congregational in organization or polity;

Third, it was, in general sympathy and brotherhood, Unitarian;

Fourth, and finally, he considered the relation of his church to other churches, both Unitarian and otherwise.

Although only in outline form, these notes suggest clearly Eliot's central ideas.

First, it was a Christian Church, that is a religious organization and not a "Lyceum, nor Benevolent Society, nor Reformer's Association, but a church — and that distinctly Christian." For Eliot the Communion Table, not the pulpit, was the center of the church.

53

Second, the congregational form and organization of the church was explained in the Church's Prayer Book, which Eliot had compiled in 1842. In an introduction to the first edition, he had given the reasons for publishing such a work, saying that its use would "materially lessen my own labors on the Sabbath and at other times — a consideration which my peculiar position compels me to regard." Also, "it will render it easier to conduct the exercise of Public Worship in the absence of a regular minister." Besides several orders of worship and a collection of hymns and psalms, the Prayer Book explained some of the organizational and doctrinal principles of the church. It notes that in the original Constitution of the church it was

> expressly provided that no Creed, or Articles of Faith, shall ever be adopted in the Church, as a test of membership, except the Bible itself. . . . Each individual is understood to be responsible for his peculiar religious opinions, not to the members of this Church, but to God and Christ alone. . . .
>
> It was chiefly on this ground that the name of *Congregational* was assumed, rather than that of any particular sect. The object was to keep this Church and Society free from all sectarian trammels, and to avoid the names which identify it with a party. So far as the constitution, or the name of the Society is concerned, the Pastor is as much at liberty to preach doctrines of the Trinitarian as of the Unitarian system. By assuming the name Congregational, this Society desires to take the broadest Christian ground, and claims to be *independent,* both in church government and in matters of faith, of every authority except that of sacred Scriptures.

It is clear from this that for Eliot the word Unitarian was decidedly an adjective, modifying the noun Christian or Christianity, so that in the outline of his doctrine of the church, its general Unitarian sympathies and affiliations are stated third after its Christian character and Congregational organization.

Fourth, and most interesting, are Eliot's definitions of Unitarianism, and on this subject his notes are most detailed.

Unitarian, he said, had a broad definition including generally all who do not believe in the Trinity. It also had a restricted, denominational identification which, though allowing for "large latitude for belief" distinctly included, at least for himself:

First, The Unity and Goodness of God;

Second, the Divine Mission and Authority of Christ, as Teacher and Redeemer;

Third, the inspiration and authority of Scripture; and

Fourth, Responsibility to God, and consequent Retribution for Sins.

While acknowledging the relative conservatism of his own Unitarianism, he said, "What binds me most closely to the Unitarian movement is not argument of opinion — that is always a weak bond and among thoughtful men the weakest — it is *agreement of Principles.*" And these Unitarian Principles were, he averred, the Rational, the Liberal and the Practical. In addition, another appeal was the intellectual and moral character of its advocates. He noted that Unitarians had no monopoly on these principles, but that they were most prominent in the Unitarian value system. Thus while holding true to the doctrines of the classical Unitarian Christianity he had learned from Channing, Eliot also held true to the Broad Church idea which allowed for considerable differences among the individual churches of the Unitarian body.

However, his personal distaste for some other expressions of Unitarianism is rather amusingly revealed in one note under "Relation to other churches," where, discussing Unitarians, he wrote:

> Not responsible for the vagaries and sophomorical eccentricities of every 6×10 church and 1×1 minister. We look with philosophic indifference upon both the

praise and blame of Theodore Parker, and are not distressed to know what Dr. Hedge meant by "Divinity of Christ."

Eliot's views on both the Christian character of Unitarianism and the wide latitude of belief permitted by its rational and liberal principles were in accord with the majority of at least the New England Unitarians of his time. In 1853 at the Annual Meeting of the American Unitarian Association in Boston, a strong re-affirmation of the Christian character of Unitarianism was passed without a dissenting vote.

But of course the fact that it was felt necessary to pass such a resolution was in itself an indication that this consensus was being challenged, as indeed it was by the Transcendentalists and others with more radical views — Emerson, Parker and Hedge among them. Many of the newer churches in the west, as might be expected, tended to less traditional views — although to this general rule the Church of the Messiah was always a most significant exception.

Nonetheless, the Church of the Messiah was for several years the main financial support, and Eliot a major leader, of the Western Unitarian Conference. Eliot was instrumental in the founding of the Conference which became the major regional organization among the Unitarians. As early as the 1840s he had seen the need for an association of the far-flung churches that lay outside the New England bastions of tradition and security. In 1849 a meeting was scheduled to establish a western conference, but Eliot was unable to attend and the attempt failed. How-ever, just three years later, in May of 1852, at a meeting which was originally to be held in St. Louis but moved to Cincinnati because the new Church of the Messiah building was not yet completed, the Western Unitarian Conference was success-fully established and Eliot elected its first President. The Church of the Messiah was the major financial contributor to the Conference in its formative years and continued substantial monetary support even after Eliot personally disassociated himself from the Conference over what was to him a matter of crucial principle.

In the last of the Lincoln-Douglas Debates, held in Alton, Illinois, on October 15, 1858, Lincoln referred to the controversy "in the Unitarian Church in this very town two years ago." He meant the sixth annual meeting of the Western Unitarian Conference held in Alton in May of 1857. The issue which divided the Conference in that year, and which lead indirectly to Eliot's withdrawal from the Conference, was of course slavery. But Eliot's primary concern was to affirm the vital principle of congregational autonomy. The larger questions raised in this debate regarding the proper role of church bodies relative to controversial social and political issues remain with us today.

According to Eliot the possibility of compromising congregational autonomy was a grave concern even as the Western Conference was initially organized in 1852:

> One fear stood in our way and embarrassed us, in the preliminary consultations, to such a degree, that we hesitated whether or not to proceed any further; namely, that an association of churches is always in danger of assuming ecclesiastical authority, or at least in proceeding in such manner as to compromise each other, and, by their associated action, to lessen or interfere with the independent, individual action of separate churches. We desired to secure full and fair discus-sion, both of doctrines and principles, in religion and morality; but to have no creed, nor statement of principles, nor expression of opinion, which would, di-rectly or indirectly, implicate those present or represented at the meetings held.

In his history of the Western Unitarian Conference, *Freedom Moves West,* Charles H. Lyttle accuses Eliot of inconsistency on this point, declaring that he was willing to support dogmatic positions for the Conference when they were in accord with his own religious beliefs. Actually, Eliot appears to have been entirely consistent in this regard, holding that the Conference was an association of independent churches which could take no doctrinal or creedal positions.

When, for example, in 1854, meeting at Louisville, the Conference received a Report on "Unitarian Views' which it had ordered previously — "Views" or doctrines acceptable to the overwhelming majority of the delegates at the meeting, including Eliot — it was he who moved a resolution of thanks receiving the Report and acknowledging that the Conference had "heard it with much profit." And then, he said:

> Resolved — however, that under our organization as the Conference of Western Unitarian Churches, we have no right to adopt any statement of belief as authoritative, or as a declaration of Unitarian Faith, other than the New Testament itself, which is the divinely authorized rule both of faith and practice.

Lyttle undoubtedly would take exception to the last part of Eliot's resolution, but at the time the reference to the New Testament was not considered dogmatic or doctrinal. In the controversy of 1857 Eliot may have been wrong, but he was not, *contra* Lyttle, inconsistent. In fact, at the time, his opponents never denied his consistency, though they disagreed with his position.

It is said that hard cases make bad law. Something parallel can be said about social justice issues and the church. "Reformers, especially when they enter the pulpit, are too apt to overlook everything except the end to be secured," Eliot said. Stirred by moral passion, principles in calmer times faithfully held are forgotten and abandoned.

The issue at Alton, in 1857, at the fifth meeting of the Western Unitarian Conference, was — for the majority who ultimately prevailed — slavery. But for Eliot and those who agreed with him the issue was whether the Conference would abandon its principle against making resolutions.

A long and fascinating account of the proceedings at the Alton meeting, written by a reporter obviously sympathetic to Eliot and his position, appeared in the Missouri *Republican*. Once the issue of slavery was raised, it said:

> Speeches waxed hot and temper. The calm waters of the Christian brotherhood were agitated and tempest-tossed. So many chafed and struggled for the floor that the fifteen minute rule for speeches was adopted. To a looker-on the change was a sad one. To the active participants, the occasion was one of an intense strife for some imaginary victory.
>
> The "Abolition" portion, who soon proved to be the strongest by at least two-thirds of the Conference, declared the action of the Conference last year, at Chicago, when they gave the slavery question the go-by, was wrong; that the Unitarian church *was* anti-slavery, and it was incumbent upon the Conference *as such* to pronounce publicly against the unholy and iniquitous system. . . .
>
> [Eliot and others] claimed that this Assembly was simply a Conference of voluntary delegations from various free and independent congregations, and it had no power to make creeds, establish platforms, or pass resolutions declaratory of Church position upon *any* of the great contested questions of the day. . . .
>
> I should state that some harsh speeches were made during these proceedings. A young man named *Conway* . . . made a violent effort, in which the Minister of God was far less discernible than the pot-house politician. Judge *Treat* [of St. Louis] became well warmed, and proceeded in his characteristic, vehement, sledge hammer style. Dr. Eliot was, as ever, smooth, courteous, forbearing, although flings and implications were plainly pointed at him, in preceding speeches. But it was evident that his stand was taken, and he, the leader of the minority, would resist, to the last, this (as he deemed) usurpation of power, which was antagonistic to the whole spirit and letter of the doctrines of the independent, free-thinking, anti-creed Unitarian church.

By the following day it was clear that the Conference would pass an anti-slavery resolution, though in an attempt to calm the tempest-tossed waters, the initial more radical resolutions were withdrawn and what was recommended was characterized by Eliot himself as a "very gentle, mild and conciliatory statement of opinion . . . to which, in itself, very few would have desired to object." "But at the same time," Eliot explained to his congregation in a sermon two weeks later

it was distinctly declared in debate, that the right to offer and pass more radical resolutions was not waived; and it was decided by the chair that the right of thus expressing itself by resolutions, on any subject, might at any time be exercised by majority vote, at the discretion of the conference.

Eliot was unwilling to vote either for or against the proposed resolution under these circumstances. When he arose to speak, according to the newspaper account:

All eyes were turned on him. A needle could have been heard to fall, as he proceeded. He was calm, clear — his voice as pleasant as the breath of a June morning. He was standing towards the front of the church, and most of us behind him, and we could not see his face. He said, in substance, that the storm had come even upon the Conference of the Unitarian church of the land. He had been one of the originators of that manner of assemblage of the Church — he little thought, *then,* that it would prove a means of usurpation upon Unitarian independence and sectional antagonism. He could not consent to the report. He denied the power of the body, except by a ruthless arbitrary vote of a small majority of members, to pass it over the protest of a minority — even a minority of one. But he saw what was about to follow. He did not object to the particular wording of the committee's report. What they had said, was said as kindly as possible. He did not object to their particular views upon the question of slavery. He had his. But he regarded this step as *the entering wedge,* and that the first step to sectional agitation, upon a theoretic question — a question which, in its practical relations, was far beyond their reach — and that hereafter, the Conference would not prove an assemblage of representatives of *all* the Unitarian churches in the land; that the action now about to be taken affected him, and his church; that it would tend to cripple his means of usefulness among his people; and, therefore, conceding to every other delegate the right of perfect freedom of action in this matter, he, for *himself* alone, without consulting with even his brother delegates from St. Louis, believed it his duty, most respectfully, to withdraw from the Conference, and asked that his name be erased from its role of membership.

It was a solemn moment.

After Judge Treat, in a few cordial remarks, made a similar announcement and request, and after Wayman Crow made a motion, which was defeated, asking that the whole matter be postponed to next year,

Hon. Robert Smith, [Congressman] of this congressional District, one of the most prominent members of the Alton Unitarian Church, now gained the floor. His feelings had not been a little ruffled the day previous by indiscreet remarks of the younger preachers, in discussing the slavery question. They had spoken sneeringly of politicians, of the public press, and had remarked that "St. Louis had already cost the Conference too much." Mr. Smith was warm — yea, it is not stretching a point to say he was thoroughly aroused. He regretted that this step was about to be taken — that resolutions were about to be passed to divide the Unitarian brotherhood of the North and South, upon a theoretic question, suspended on an imaginary line. . . . He would say to those young advocates of *liberty* (the fast young preachers) that they could quite as well show their anti-slavery zeal to the world, by going to the slave States, and live among, and deal with, and preach against it, as had Dr. Eliot for many years past, as to enter such a body as this, and make empty speeches and pass imaginary thunderbolts in the way of resolutions, against an evil which here did not exist. . . .

And thus the controversy raged on. But there was never any real question about the result. With the adoption of the anti-slavery resolution, as the newspaper report concluded, the "Unitarian Church of the United States was divided."

And soon the nation would be divided as well.

Second church building, Northwest corner of Ninth and Olive
Dedicated December 7, 1851
(Courtesy First Unitarian Church Archives)

MISCELLANY, 1858–1861

"Few buildings anywhere can excel in massiveness and beauty, the 'Church of the Messiah' on Olive Street, under the pastoral charge of Mr. Eliot. This house and grounds is said to have cost $100,000, and yet there is nothing gaudy about it; it is built of brick and iron, of which metal there was used in the construction of this noble edifice some seventy tons of pig iron. It is of very imposing appearance; the material is the very best hard brick, with heavy grouted walls, on the construction of which no pains or expense was spared — every part built to last for ages, to go down to posterity as a monument to be admired. We have never witnessed such extra pains in securing a good and excellent job, as was manifested in the creation of this large edifice. It was not built by contract, but all the material was selected by the committee, and all parts done under their supervision by the workmen employed for the purpose. The ground plat is about ninety by some one hundred and twenty feet, and about seventy feet high, surmounted by a beautifully proportioned spire one hundred and sixty-seven feet high. The internal finish corresponds with the external, and is really beautiful, tasteful, yet devoid of glitter or mere show."

— *from the* Sketch Book of St. Louis, *1858*

* * *

"Frankly speaking I must say for myself that the experience of that [1857 meeting of the Western Unitarian] Conference will probably keep me from all attempt at associated action hereafter; for if the checks and guards were insufficient there to prevent violation of the Congregational principle, no one can ever feel safe. I do not think I should rejoin the Conference, even if you were "to have the magnanimity" to pass a "Penitet me" Resolution. . . . Our church here will not be "represented," but undoubtedly Mr. Staples [Associate Pastor of the Church of the Messiah] and, I hope, a good many others will be at Quincy. . . . The year is a bad one for raising money. . . . This is going to be a great city, *I believe,* and we need to lay very broad foundations for the Educational and charitable institutions, as a proper provision for the future. A big work for a little band — but they who are "co-workers" with Him can gradually succeed in doing His work."

— *WGE to James Freeman Clarke, April 9, 1860*

* * *

"My own opinion is that we shall never have a Unitarian church of real religious strength until we join to the unqualified preaching of the Divine Unity, an equally unqualified preaching of the Divine Son-ship of Christ. The *essential* Evangelical doctrines must be brought back into our church, or they will die. We *cannot* believe in the Trinity, but we can believe in Divine help, in mediational agency, in the necessity of Christ to the Soul. At least I can. . . . But I do not feel equal to a theological contest, and therefore hesitate from printing anything which is likely to elicit comment."

— *WGE to Edward Everett Hale, November 1, 1860*

* * *

"Political affairs at the South look badly; but the noise will end in a sputter. I wish South Carolina would or could go out and stay out. South Carolina and Massachusetts are the mischief makers."

— WGE Notebook, November 12, 1860

*　　　*　　　*

"Gave a written memoranda of my thinking [to Amos Tucker of New Hampshire], which he will show to Mr. Lincoln. It is not likely to have any effect, but I feel bound to try, what little I can, to keep the peace."

— WGE Notebook, January 8, 1861

*　　　*　　　*

CHAPTER IV
LOYALTY AND RELIGION (1861)

"I must preach another Union Natural sermon, to free my own mind: to clear my own conscience."

On December 21, 1860, the Rev. Thomas Lamb Eliot, eldest son of William Greenleaf Eliot, after several months abroad for reasons of health, arrived in New York City, where he found a terse telegram from his father awaiting him: "The times are out of joint. Come home as soon as possible."

The day before, South Carolina had passed an ordinance of secession, and it was evident that other Southern states would soon follow suit. The Border State of Missouri was, within itself, as conflicted as the nation as a whole; and the City of St. Louis represented in microcosm the divisions and tensions of the entire country. Close friends of long standing would no longer even greet one another on the street. Members of the same St. Louis families enlisted in the opposing armies. Slaves and slave-holders, freemen and mulattoes, Yankee tradesmen and European immigrants, Southern belles and frontierswomen — St. Louis in 1861 was a cosmopolitan hodgepodge of all these and more.

For the minister who still felt that the whole city was his parish, this would be a time of personal anguish as well as public concern. The time would shortly come when he would watch a large number of his parishioners walk out of the church on a Sunday morning, many of them never to return. And more than once he must have tested the limits of the injunction to love the sinner even as we hate the sin.

On May 24, 1857, Eliot preached a sermon entitled "Social Reform" in which he had explained to his congregation his reasons for withdrawing from the Western Unitarian Conference during the controversy at the Alton meeting discussed in the last chapter. The sermon is an excellent summary of Eliot's position on the proper relation of the church to political and social issues. On the subject of *Political Preaching* Eliot had this to say:

> The introduction of politics into the pulpit is almost always unfortunate, because very few preachers are good politicians; and also, because, by assuming the position of a partisan, the preacher must necessarily give offence to many of his

people, and will generally lose a part of the best influence belonging to his office. They who come to church seek for, or at least need, religious instruction, consolation and guidance; and to offer them a disquisition on party politics, is, "instead of bread to give them a stone; instead of fish, a scorpion." They come, already weary of that sort of strife, and desirous of hearing words of peace and rest; to retreat from newspaper warfare and congressional harangues; to refresh themselves with words of Gospel soberness and truth. They have therefore a right to complain, if, for a sermon, they hear a political speech, and are thus compelled to employ their minds with a continuation of worldly vexation and care. If the clergyman feels it his absolute duty to discuss questions of constitutional law and judicial authority, and the like, let him do so on the week day at the political meeting, as a citizen; not on the Sabbath, as a religious teacher, in the pulpit. Such is, at least, the general rule. There may be exceptions, and have been, as in revolutionary times, or at some great social crisis; but the minister of Jesus Christ, whose "kingdom is not of this world," should shun such occasions rather than seek them.

To the general rule, then, there might be exceptions, as "at some great crisis." In 1861, the crisis at hand, Eliot showed little hesitancy to use the pulpit to express his political convictions.

Even before secession was a reality, Eliot had affirmed his position as an Unconditional Union man in his Thanksgiving Day sermon in 1860. And on January 27, 1861, he addressed directly the issue of secession as it was then before the voters of Missouri in a sermon entitled, "The Higher Law Doctrine North and South." In it he noted that the so-called "appeal to a higher law" was employed by the extremists of both sides, Northern radicals (Abolitionists) and Southern Secessionists, to justify defiance of the law. The real issue for Eliot was the dissolution of the Union. "All over the land," he said, "the question of disunion is freely discussed — a word which we ought not to hear without shuddering." To him the consequences were evident and dire:

As it looks to me from the teachings of history, from our knowledge of human nature, and from the angry passions already working, both at the North and the South, the question to be discussed may involve not only disunion, but social disorganization, civil commotion, civil war, servile war, anarchy, military despotism, national ruin. It may be to decide upon the destruction of the grandest republic the world has ever seen; upon the continued success or total failure of the great experiment of American freedom.

This sermon was well received, published and widely circulated. But the tide of circumstance and sentiment was running strongly in the other direction. Lincoln was inaugurated on March 4. Five weeks later, on April 12, Fort Sumter was fired upon. In Missouri when the Legislature convened on May 2, Governor Claiborne F. Jackson, a strong Secessionist from the beginning, recommended that Missouri unite herself with the other slave states, including the raising of armed forces, and urged the passage of a military bill which would confer on himself almost dictatorial powers to resist Federal authority. The bill passed.

Under these circumstances a provisional state government was established to preserve Missouri's nominal loyalty to the Union, with Hamilton R. Gamble as Governor. Eliot estimated that "two thirds of the people of the State are disloyal, and a large number of the remainder inactive."

"The rebels seem determined to force Missouri from the Union by first making it impossible for Union men to live here," he said, and: "Nothing but a strong army of occupation can hold the state and prevent its social destruction."

Such was the state of affairs when Eliot wrote in his journal in mid-August, "I must preach another Union Natural sermon, to free my own mind, to clear my own conscience." He preached the sermon on August 16, and it was published a few days later under the title "Loyalty and Religion." The burden of his argument was that religion and patriotism both required the same actions and occasioned the same duties under the present circumstances. Subtitled "A Discourse for the Times," Eliot began the sermon by again stressing his reluctance to preach on such subjects and his reason for now doing so:

Religion and law are the great conservative influences of society. The teachers of religion, like the administrators of law, are naturally and properly upon the conservative side. They are bound to the advocacy of peace and good order. They are the natural opponents of violence and revolutionary change. Only under the plainest arguments of necessity, can they properly become agitators and disturbers of established rule.

But the same reasons which should make the minister of Christ conservative, and which have generally led me to exclude from the pulpit the excitements of political discussion, seem to me to require plain and earnest speech, at a time like this. . . . We desire to speak dispassionately, and I know that as to the different steps in this progress of events, diversity of opinion exists. But this general statement of the question at issue may be made, in the fairness of which all will concur: First, that the whole country is in the condition of civil war, the object of which is, on the one side, to accomplish a Revolution by separating a part of the States from the Government of the United States; and, on the other, to resist, and if possible, prevent such a result. And secondly, in our own State, it is a struggle to determine whether we shall remain in the Union or go out of it. . . .

Now, I assume that, in such a case, no one who loves his country, or has any interest in its welfare, can or ought to be silent. . . .

I know that some of you differ from me as to the propriety of introducing the subject, in this place. It is urged that offense will be given, that it is impolitic and unwise. But it is not a matter of policy, nor choice, with me; not of mere conventional propriety and taste: not of praise or blame. It is a matter of positive obligation. I may do no good, but I must try. No man can answer to his country, to his conscience, to his God, who does not do his best, however little that may be. My convictions are too strong to be repressed. From the abundance of the heart the mouth will speak, and is very like to speak plainly.

Having thus argued that it was not only his choice but his duty to speak, he went on to say that greatest problem in the public mind was its slowness in recognizing the magnitude and importance of the present struggle and controversy. In his own mind the issue could not be greater:

It is the existence or non-existence of our country. The permanence or dismemberment of a great nation. "Republican institutions are on their trial, and according to the result, will the verdict of the world be given." The plain question is, shall we be one, strong, united people, or scattered into, no one can tell how many communities, republics or monarchies, at strife among ourselves, the scorn and contempt of the nations. . . .

I am a lover of peace; I am now, and always have been, its advocate. In social, religious and civil affairs I have always been ready to plead for it. Among the benedictions, no one do I covet more than that upon the peacemakers. While, therefore, I do not assume to decide whether or not the present civil war was unavoidable, I am thankful that the responsibility did not and does not rest upon me. I did all I could to prevent it, and would do anything in my power to bring it to a just and righteous close. So much I feel bound to say, for I cannot appear as the general advocate of war, even when the progress of events compels me reluctantly to accept it, as the last appeal.

Nevertheless, leaving the responsibility of the beginning and continuance of this conflict to those upon whom it must rest, I feel equally bound to say, that beyond all the evils of the present war, with all its calamities, losses, sufferings and sins, would be the loss of national existence, the permanent severance of the American Union. . . . Whether the present war continues one year or ten, it is not so bad as the continued series of wars and internal strifes that would certainly succeed the disruption of the Union. . . .

The question now before us is not to determine upon war or peace. This has already been determined. . . . The only thing left for individuals to do is to choose on which side they will stand. We speak with sadness, and the stern reality of passing events is yet more sad. For weeks, for months, perhaps for years, this fearful civil war is destined to go on. But if it results, at last, as God grant it may, in the full re-establishment of the United States government in its integrity and pristine vigor, the sacrifice will have been well endured, the suffering will not have been in vain.

Nor do I speak as one who has himself nothing to lose. Few persons, perhaps, have more or greater interests at stake than I. Whatever I possess — not much, but all that I desire, enough for my perfect contentment and that of my family — is in exactly such a position, that either the "secession" of the State, or a long continuance of war, would make it absolutely worthless. But that is a comparatively small matter. My interest in the general prosperity goes much deeper than this. My life, my happiness, my hopes, whether of usefulness or enjoyment, are so intertwined with the prosperity of St. Louis, that I have no thoughts beyond. To meet with failure here, is to have failed in the work of life. This Church, in which a whole generation has grown up under my care, and which is to me my home, my family, friends and kindred, at once the place of working and the haven of rest, for which I am willing to spend and be spent, and in which I have found, through so many years of trial, so many friends and helpers, faithful as brothers and true as steel; the charities of the church, by which hundreds of children are rescued from vice, and hundreds of families shielded from hunger and cold; the various charitable and benevolent institutions of the city, in all of which we have labored to do our proper and more than our proportionate share; the educational enterprises, large in design and successful in their prosecution, already established, as we had fondly hoped, beyond the possibility of failure; these things, together with whatever else belongs to the associations and labors of twenty-seven years of severe yet happy experience, the fruits of a life not idly spent — do they not stand as "hostages given to fortune," binding me to labor for the welfare of this community, for the city in which we live? During the last ten years, this congregation of the Church of the Messiah has contributed, in various works of benevolence and charity, not less than the sum of $50,000 annually, and we had our hopes and plans to do as much in every year to come. These are interests not lightly to be sacrificed, and to any one who knows how to value the uses of life, they stand higher than considerations of personal advantage or gain. But so far as I have, or may hereafter have, to do with them, I would cheerfully see them scattered to the four winds, to begin over again the work of my life, here or elsewhere, under all the disadvantages of impaired health and advancing years, with this one hope to sustain me, that the sacrifice would, in some small degree, contribute to the maintenance of unimpaired national existence, the restoration of the American Union to its former strength.

Do you call this sentimental patriotism? It is not so. It is but the just and reasonable love of country, which every man should cherish, and without which honesty is seldom long maintained. The love of country, loyalty, patriotism, is the foundation of all social virtues, the corner stone on which society is built. It lies deeper than filial duty or parental love; it is more sacred than the domestic tie. He who loves father or mother, wife or children, so much as to become a traitor to his country, is a weak and miserable man. A poet has truly said, "he who loves not his country cannot love anything." It is the virtue which last forsakes the heart of a bad man, and that which adds crowning excellence to the character of the good. . . . It stands next to religion; and the man who betrays his country can hardly be true to his God. I do not ask the man who has lost his patriotism to be my friend, for I should not know how to trust him who lacks this foundation of trustworthiness. I would not live in a community whose patriotism is dead, for it would not be worth working for, nor capable of improvement. . . .

Referring to the specifics of the current situation, he said:

At present, the great battle for the Union is here [in Missouri]. If Missouri were permanently lost to the Union, it would be an irreparable blow, and the strength of the Government would be effectually broken. Commanding, as she does, the mouth of the Ohio and of the Illinois, the Upper Mississippi and the whole of the Missouri River, lying on the highway to Kansas, the gold regions and the Pacific Ocean, and possessed of inestimable mineral resources, Missouri is a military, commercial and political necessity to the United States Government. . . .

What then shall we do? How manifest allegiance, and resist revolution? There is but one answer, which equally applies to all: We should give our whole, undivided influence, by word and deed, to sustain the cause of the United States, *by holding our own State in the Union.* That is our proper and sufficient work at the present time, which will task all our energies to accomplish. . . .

At the end of the sermon he enumerated the individual's various duties — as an American, as a Missourian, as a citizen. He then concluded:

Finally, and including all, we have duties as Christians. War is not Christian work, and the time will come for its abolition, as for that of all other social wrongs and evils. But it has not come yet, and under an existing state of war our Christian duties remain not less than in time of peace. John the Baptist gave rules of conduct to the soldiers who came to him, and the Saviour, and his apostles after him, received the Roman Centurions among their disciples. I hold it to be a Christian duty to defend our country from invasion and rebellion, peaceably if we can, forcibly if we must. Otherwise society would be completely in the hands of the wicked, and social progress would be impossible. There is also a difference in the conduct of warfare, and we may make it a war of barbarism, or of comparative humanity and civilization. There is danger, particularly in this State, where such personal, vindictive feelings have been aroused, that all humanity will be forgotten and savage warfare take its place. Let us do our part to keep Christian principles alive. Remember that among our opponents, for every one designing and scheming man, there are many sincere and many hundreds deceived and mistaken. Do not forget that we are fighting against our own countrymen, and we shall then stand ready for the first moment of fair and just settlement which may come. It is one thing to be decided, energetic, resolute; quite another to be vindictive, overbearing, blood-thirsty. There are no circumstances in life, under which a Christian may not do his whole duty. Our duty as patriots and our duty as Christians must be done, if at all, at one and the same time. "Render therefore unto Caesar the things that are Caesar's, and unto God the things that are God's." The seeming conflict of duties will end in the noblest service that can be rendered by man.

Notwithstanding Eliot's call to charity among those who differed, some walked out before the conclusion of the sermon, and many never returned to the Church of the Messiah. One of Eliot's sons, Henry Ware Eliot, in an unpublished reminiscence, personalized some of the conflicts and deep feelings which were aroused:

Among the most bitter [about Eliot's position] were Dr. William Carr Lane and his family. [William Carr Lane had been the first Mayor of St. Louis.] He had been our family physician for years and was a close friend. Edward Appleton, father's cousin, and his wife Kate (Provost) utterly ignored us. She was mother's brides-maid and met her future husband in St. Louis when she was visiting our house. She was of a southern family, Quakers, and was intensely "secesh." *He* was governed entirely by her. He was ashamed to speak to father, who always insisted on stopping him in the street to shake hands. *She* publicly stated that she was carrying a pistol and "would shoot either Mr. Yeatman or Mr. Eliot if either spoke to her."

The Eliots were living at this time in the Beaumont Cottage, a residence located on what was then the outskirts of the city. Soldier's of Gratz Brown's regiment were quartered nearby, in Uhrig's Cave, which led to several incidents. Eliot filed a formal complaint after one particular morning when several volleys of rifle shots were fired at his fence while he and his family were inside. Henry Ware

Eliot relates a more humorous occurrence around the same time. The nearby soldiers were a great nuisance because they

> constantly came over the fence into our premises to steal fruit. One summer evening we heard them shaking the trees and father, Tom, and I ran down in the orchard to drive them away. When we got among the trees, the men had scattered and we supposed that they had all left. In order to frighten them, father fired a revolver straight upwards. Instantly, a man fell from the tree overhead and begged us to spare his life. I doubt if he was nearly as much frightened as father, who thought he had shot him. But the man was not hurt. He gave his name and was permitted to depart. But father unloaded his revolver and gave it away the next day. He would never touch one afterward.

The war affected every aspect of life. No individual and no institution was unaffected, and of course this included the ongoing projects of the Church of the Messiah.

On April 12, the day Sumter was fired upon, there appeared in the newspapers a series of police orders related to the emerging crisis, several of them focussed especially on limiting, actually abrogating, the rights of Negroes. A Sunday School for Negroes called "Nigirita" had been meeting in the Library Room of the Church of the Messiah for about five years, under the direction of Callie Kasson, a member of the church. It had over 100 pupils. Under the terms of the new police orders it would have had to be disbanded as "an unlawful assembly," but Eliot was able to obtain a permit for its continued operation.

In May Eliot wrote a letter to the trustees of the Church suggesting a reduction in the level of pew rentals and a corresponding schedule of salary reductions for himself and the other staff of the church, "the reasons for this being too evident, in the state of the times, to need recapitulation."

Similarly, in June his schedule of salary proposals for the Washington University Directors included the statement that all positions were conditional upon the ability of the University to continue in full operation. These were still the University's formative years; the first college class would not be graduated until 1862. The fledgling school could easily have become another casualty of the war. That it was not is simply another indication of the dedication of its founders. Eliot himself, in addition to the other duties and responsibilities which fell upon him in these years, volunteered his services gratuitously as Professor of Metaphysics, as a means of reducing University expenses, which at this time were still being borne almost entirely by members of the church.

Still, even with such efforts, Eliot despaired of the future of the school. Beside the newspaper notices of the fall terms of Washington University and Mary Institute on August 29, which he posted in his Notebook, he wrote in a large hand, "Alas! I fear the Institutions will scarcely live."

Eliot believed that for geographical and logistical reasons, Missouri was of extreme strategic importance to both sides. He had detailed some of the reasons for this in his sermon in August. He elaborated them more fully in a long letter to the Secretary of the Treasury, Salmon P. Chase, about the military situation in Missouri, asking Chase to "Lay my letter before the President if you consider it worthy of such regard." Urging additional troops for the State, he wrote in part:

> I claim to be better informed than the majority of our citizens of the actual number and condition of troops here; my interest in the hospitals and sick has led me to visit the camps and observe the men both as to numbers and discipline, and I assure you, sir, that if you consider the importance of this state to the Union, and the disloyalty of its citizens, and the manifest eagerness of the slave power to keep it, we have not one half the strength we need. Missouri once lost could not be recovered, and its loss would be an almost fatal blow to the North.

"Pardon my intrusion," he concluded this letter: "My whole heart is in this cause.

The war of barbarism against civilization, of slavery against freedom, is the great event of the nineteenth century. May God protect the right!"

As indicated in this letter, Eliot was already by this time involved with military hospitals and the care of the wounded. Such work was carried out during the Civil War under the auspices of the Western Sanitary Commission (and the United States Sanitary Commission), a tremendous voluntary enterprise headquartered in St. Louis in which Eliot played a leading role.

In the first year of the war some 60 battles or major skirmishes were fought in Missouri. At the outset of the war the government was entirely unprepared for the medical care of the large army suddenly called into being. For example, a report on the history of the Western Sanitary Commission relates the scene as, a week or so after a battle near Springfield, Missouri, the sick and wounded began to arrive in St. Louis:

> The battle of Wilson's Creek was fought on August 10th, twelve miles south of Springfield, near the Fayetteville Road. This was one of the most desperately fought engagements of the war, and the number of wounded was very great. The wounded, numbering 721, were brought all the way from Springfield to Rolla in ambulances and army wagons, and thence by cars to Saint Louis, and so little preparation had then been made for such an event that there were no additional hospital accommodations for so many in the whole city. The "New House of Refuge Hospital," situated two miles south of St. Louis, had only been opened on the 6th of the same month, by Medical Director De Camp, with Dr. Bailley in charge, two excellent and humane surgeons of the regular army, and was as yet unfinished and unprovided with the requisites of a good hospital. Its condition at the time is thus described in an article in the North American Review for April, 1864, entitled "Loyal Work in Missouri." "It had neither stoves, nor bedsteads, nor beds, nor bedding, nor food, nor nurses, nor any thing prepared. The first hundred arrived at night. They had been brought in wagons a hundred and twenty miles, over a rough road, by hurried marches, suffering for food and water, from Springfield to Rolla, and thence by rail to Saint Louis to the station on Fourteenth Street. There, having had nothing to eat for ten hours, they were put into furniture carts (much better than those instruments of torture called ambulances) and carried the remaining three miles. Bare walls, bare floors, and an empty kitchen received them; but the kind-hearted surgeon, Bailley, did all he could to make kindness take the place of good fare. He obtained from the neighbors cooked food for their supper, and lost no time in getting together the various means of comfort. The poor fellows were so shattered and travel-worn that they were thankful enough to get eatable food, with the hard boards to sleep upon, and no word of complaint did we ever hear one of them utter. In the course of the week three or four hundred more were brought in, the condition of things meanwhile rapidly improving; but so great was the difficulty of obtaining anything that was wanted, that many of the badly wounded men lay there in the same unchanged garments in which they had been brought from the battle-field three weeks before.

Immediately after this, Eliot began to develop ideas for a Sanitary Commission to deal with the care of the wounded and the spiritual well-being of the soldiers. Dorothea Dix had visited the Eliots in St. Louis in February. She was the General Superintendent of the Nurses of Military Hospitals in the United States, and Eliot's plan was that she would direct the selection and appointment of women nurses for the Commission; he brought her back to St. Louis soon after it was established. Eliot and Miss Dix remained close friends until her death some years after the end of the war.

In the last days of August, Eliot communicated his ideas for a Sanitary Commission informally with a number of people, including Major General John C. Fremont, who was then in command of the Western armies, and his wife, Jessie

Benton Fremont. Both encouraged him to go forward. So on September 3, he drafted in his journal a series of "suggestions" for the creation of a Western Sanitary Commission, naming himself and four other men as the Board of a voluntary civilian commission. As Eliot proposed it, operating under the direction of the Army's Medical Director, the Commission would have the authority

> to select, fit up and furnish suitable buildings for Army and Brigade Hospitals, in such places and in such manner as circumstances require. It will attend to the selection and appointment of women nurses, under the authority and by the direction of Miss D. L. Dix, General Superintendent of the Nurses of Military Hospitals in the United States. It will cooperate with the surgeons of the several hospitals in providing male nurses, and in whatever manner practicable, and by their consent. It shall have the authority to visit the different camps, to consult with the commanding officers, and the colonels and other officers of the several regiments, with regard to the sanitary and general condition of the troops, and aid them in providing proper means for the preservation of health and prevention of sickness, by supply of wholesome and well cooked food, by good systems of drainage, and other practicable methods. It will obtain from the community at large such additional means of increasing the comfort and promoting the moral and social welfare of the men, in camp and hospital, as may be needed, and cannot be furnished by Government Regulations. It will from time to time, report directly to the Commander-in-Chief of the Department the condition of the camps and hospitals, with such suggestions as can properly be made by a Sanitary Board.

Two days later Eliot drafted these suggestions, they were copied verbatim by Mrs. Fremont and endorsed by her husband; and on September 10 they were formally issued as Special Order #159. Thus quickly was the Western Sanitary Commission created. Appointed by this order, as designated by Eliot, were four prominent lay members of the Church of the Messiah: James E. Yeatman, President; Carlos S. Greeley, Treasurer; Dr. J. B. Johnson, George Partridge, and Eliot himself.

Predictably, Eliot wasted no time before drafting "An Appeal to the Public" for funds and supplies, which was signed by the members of the Commission and Board and published on September 16. Nor did Eliot limit his appeal to local sources. On September 20, there appeared in the Boston *Evening Transcript* an appeal addressed "To the Patriotic Women of New England," signed by Eliot on behalf of the Western Sanitary Commission. An editorial in the same issue of the paper urged that the appeal be met with a "hearty response" and added, "Dr. Eliot is one of the most influential citizens of Missouri and is widely known throughout the country for his zeal on behalf of every good word and work."

It is not generally recognized that there were two separate and distinct Sanitation Commissions established and operating during the Civil War. A Unitarian minister figured prominently in each organization. The United States Sanitary Commission, centered in Washington, was headed by the Rev. Henry Whitney Bellows, Minister of the All Souls Unitarian Church in New York City and one of the most powerful and influential Unitarian ministers of the time. Though the two ministers were alike in many ways — strikingly similar in their theological conservatism and in their capacity for building strong institutions — Bellows was as egotistical as Eliot was modest. As President of the United States Commission, Bellows seemed to look upon its successes as almost personal accomplishments. Much of Eliot's work was behind the scenes, and he was only too willing to let others take credit for what were mainly his own efforts. For example, many of the letters and documents which went on the public record over the name of James E. Yeatman, President of the Western Sanitary Commission, were in fact written by Eliot. Such an action by Bellows is unimaginable.

Given this aspect of Bellows' personality, it is not hard to imagine that he regarded the establishment of a second, separate, Western Sanitary Commission as an affront. He also believed that a second organization would mean an unnecessary rivalry and a less efficient operation. So, very shortly after Fremont's Special Order #159 was issued, the United States Sanitary Commission filed a formal protest against the formation of a Western Sanitary Commission and requested that such a group be made a branch of the National Commission.

For his part Eliot, who if he had personal feelings similar to Bellows' kept them well hidden, believed that the exigencies of the situation made a separate organization in the West desirable. In smaller part this reflected his general philosophic view: "Independence and individuality of action should always be kept if possible, and when lost, no excellence of system can take their place." In larger part his desire to maintain the independence of the Western Sanitary Commission was based on the extreme turmoil and difficulty of the situation in St. Louis and in Missouri at the time, circumstances which were not appreciated or understood even by the President or the War Department. "Not one-fourth of the city's wealthy and influential classes were loyal to the Union," Eliot later wrote, and according to him "one half of the cannon planted on the forts for the defense of the city were pointed *at* the city, to keep in awe the enemies within." Whether this was a literal or figurative image, Eliot described the earliest work of the Sanitary Commission as having to be undertaken almost in secrecy, for initially there was suspicion and even contempt for those willing to undertake any work — even that of hygiene and health — in support of the war effort.

Whatever the real motivations of the ministerial leaders of the two organizations, when the independent status of the Western Sanitary Commission was challenged by Bellows' group in October of 1861, it was Eliot who went to Washington in response. His journal is typically silent about the details, but he had a number of meetings there on the subject, including one, possibly two, with President Lincoln. The result of these meetings was that the continued existence of the Western Sanitary Commission as an independent organization was assured, and on Eliot's return to St. Louis he drafted a series of resolutions which were adopted by the Board of the Western Sanitary Commission and sent to Bellows. With them Eliot enclosed a cover letter to Bellows reaffirming the independent status of the Western Commission, and he wrote a similar letter to Secretary of War Cameron. Both letters, though written by Eliot, were signed by James Yeatman, as President, following what would become a familiar procedure.

On his return trip from Washington, Eliot had stopped briefly in Cincinnati. While he was there a local newspaper reported that he had gone to Washington "for the purpose of personally communicating with the President upon the subject of General Fremont's removal [as Commander of the Union Forces of the West]." The report said that Eliot had met twice with Lincoln and had "remonstrated against the contemplated removal."

When this report was reprinted in the St. Louis newspapers, Eliot asked for (and probably himself wrote) a retraction notice that appeared the following day and which emphasized the total insignificance of Eliot's meetings with the President.

It was typical of Eliot to attempt to hide his use of personal influence, but his interest in the subject of Fremont's potential removal as Commander of the Western Armies was well known — at least to his friends. Anonymously, he had published in *The Republican* only two weeks before a long defense of Fremont, an article entitled "General Fremont — Will He Succeed?" It is hardly credible that in a meeting between Lincoln who was under strong pressure to remove Fremont and Eliot, one of the most respected citizens of St. Louis, and one who had a strong personal interest in the situation, the subject had not been discussed. Eliot may even have learned at that time, or at least guessed, that the President's decision had already been made; Fremont was in fact relieved of his command less than two weeks later.

Though Fremont served in command only four months, with considerable question raised about his capabilities as a military leader, his brief tenure was marked by at least two significant events. One was the establishment of the Western Sanitary Commission, in which his wife Jessie Benton Fremont played a prominent role. The other was Fremont's issuance of an Emancipation Proclamation, granting freedom to the slaves of disloyal masters in Missouri. Eliot applauded this action as "the beginning of the end," and was disappointed when the order was revoked by Lincoln. Lincoln's revocation was appropriate, as Fremont had beyond question vastly exceeded his authority in issuing the order, but Eliot, who had counseled patience regarding abolition before the war, was now impatient for its achievement. He called Lincoln's revocation of Fremont's order the greatest mistake he ever made. So zealous and passionate were his words and actions during the war years that they caused his long-time friend, James Freeman Clarke, to comment in 1863, that "Eliot . . . conservative all his days, has become so radical in his reforms and all his blessed ministries that he thinks he has never been anything but a radical all his life." Others have said that his enthusiasm for Fremont's emancipation order and reaction to its revocation "showed that at heart he was more radical than conservative."

Actually, Eliot's position as both a moral and a practical man seems fairly consistent. Notwithstanding the fact that he had to endure the provocations of Northern radicals who opposed slavery from a safe distance and felt similarly free to question his moral integrity, Eliot's abhorrence of slavery was authentic and deep — as deep as the peculiar institution itself was imbedded in the fabric of the society in which he lived. Eliot's hatred of slavery was as absolute as his faith in the ultimate triumph of righteousness. He believed that true moral progress always occurs slowly. If he long counseled patience — too long for some — it was because he hoped that slavery could be gradually eliminated without paying the price of civil war. But once it became clear that the payment of that price was inevitable, no moral conflict remained; and indeed from that moment Eliot spoke and acted as fervently as the most ardent abolitionist. As a moral man, he was a radical; as a practical man, he was a conservative. In both respects he reflected his Puritan ancestry.

The great new work undertaken in 1861 was, of course, the Western Sanitary Commission. Anything like a complete record of its work would be a fair-sized book in itself. The scope and amount of work accomplished by Eliot and his four colleagues on the Board seems almost phenomenal, and certainly much of it must be credited to the countless and nameless others, men and women, who contributed to the effort in one form or another.

Beginning almost from nothing, the Commission built hospitals providing thousands of beds; food, clothing and medical supplies for the soldiers; so-called "floating hospitals" on the rivers; and small mobile hospitals, primitive forerunners of what were later called M*A*S*H units. Supplies and money poured into the Commission office on Chestnut Street, contributed from all over the country. As he had done before and would do again, Eliot turned especially to the people of Boston for support. No doubt the competition of the two Sanitary Commissions created some conflict, but the people responded generously to both.

In 1862 Eliot went to Boston to press his appeal, which resulted in contributions exceeding $50,000, and when James Yeatman later made a trip to Boston on behalf of the Commission he wrote back to Eliot: "I find that to know or be a friend of Dr. Eliot is the best of passports, both to the hearts as well as the pockets of the good people of Boston."

The Final Report of the Western Sanitary Commission enumerated contributions of over four million items, ranging from bedsteads (1,140) to bandages (114,241), from 70 cows to 206,159 gallons of sauerkraut, with an estimated value of three and a half million dollars. Many of these contributions, and cash contributions as well, were the direct results of Eliot's appeals in the East, and particularly Boston. Notwithstanding Eliot's characteristic modesty, his name became even more strongly associated with good works and the cause of the West through his efforts for the Western Sanitary Commission during the Civil War.

But even before the war had formally ended, Eliot would return to Boston, with yet another cause and another appeal to the hearts and the pockets of the good people of Boston.

MISCELLANY, 1862–1864

"Here in St. Louis, the hospitals are tolerably full — say twenty-two hundred inmates in all. . . . The sick and wounded prisoners have been a great burden — six hundred of them at one time [and they have] all been treated in hospitals like our own men. I hope your Boston women will not find fault with us for using their gifts, for a time, in this way. It is done 'by order of Gen. Halleck,' and of a greater than he, who said, 'I was sick and in prison, and ye came to me.' After all, a sick or wounded rebel, in bed and dying, looks very much like a man."

— *WGE, in a letter, later published, March 25, 1862*

*   *   *

". . . I fear, through too great desire to *use* life, I
Have not at any time learned thoroughly to enjoy it."

— *WGE, letter, April 6, 1862*

*   *   *

" 'Here,' said a student to Casaubon as they entered the old Hall of the Sorbonne, 'is a building in which men have disputed for more than four hundred year.' 'And,' said Casaubon, 'what has been settled?' "

— *from WGE's notes for his Commencement Address, 1862*

*   *   *

"In presenting a new interest and a new claim for your consideration in times like these, I feel the need of your kindest and most friendly indulgence.

"The office of soliciting (some persons would call it by a harsher name) is never one to be coveted. It is always painful, not unfrequently repulsive. It has no charms or attractions whatever; and nothing but a sense of duty in a good cause, could, under present circumstances, have impelled me to undertake it. . . .

"There are so many claims before us which belong to the time, created by the exigencies of war, and which must be met at all events, that the establishment of a University on the banks of the Mississippi, twelve hundred miles off, may well appear, at first sight, a matter of secondary and remote interest, which belongs to other people, and can quietly be set aside to wait its turn. The success of my appeal depends upon answering this fair and natural objection. I must prove to you that this is an exceptional case, which not only justifies but requires exceptional treatment. I must present before you a work of unquestionable and rare importance, which is not of merely local or sectional interest, but which belongs to the cause of liberal culture, polite learning, enlarged humanity, and by the accomplishment of which we shall do a work of Christian philanthropy, of patriotism — strictly speaking, a national work. For the establishment of a University, upon the broad foundation of unsectarian Christian principles, in a region like the Valley of the Mississippi, the central region of the United States, whose population is destined hereafter to give tone and character, whether for good or evil, to the political existence of the whole country, may well be called a Christian enterprise; and its success will be an enduring national benefit. The blotting-out of Harvard University would be a loss, not only to Massachusetts and New England, but to the nation and the civilized world.

"The work which we have undertaken, and already brought to the point of almost certain success, is the establishment at St. Louis of a University which shall be to the whole Valley of the Mississippi what Harvard University has been to New England, and which shall hold a place with her, as a daughter to a mother, in the Republic of Learning. . . ."

> — *from the printed version of Eliot's 1864 appeal*
> *to the people and churches of Boston in support*
> *of an endowment for Washington University*

*   *   *

Eliot's study at 2660 Washington Avenue
(Courtesy Washington University Archives)

CHAPTER V
FROM CHANCEL TO CHANCELLOR (1870)

"There is no such word as fail."

In his lifetime William Greenleaf Eliot made three trips to Europe. These were undertaken in major part for recuperation from exhaustion and the general debility which seems to have afflicted Eliot throughout his life. The trips were taken with the blessing and encouragement of his congregation, which recognized them as a necessity to their pastor's health even though they entailed his absence from the pulpit of up to a year or more in each case.

During his first trip abroad in 1847, as detailed in Chapter I, he was elected General Secretary of the American Unitarian Association, but declined the office and returned to St. Louis with an even stronger commitment to his ministry there than his seemingly absolute initial commitment in 1834. The two years following his return were both productive and eventful, as outlined in Chapter II; 1849 was a year of crisis in St. Louis. They took their toll on Eliot's health and strength to such an extent that just three years after his return from his first trip he left St. Louis again, and during this ten-month absence went abroad a second time.

Returning from this trip to St. Louis in October of 1851, he had written in his journal that he was only

> *too* thankful to be once more at home, among my own people. It has been a long, long year, and is the last of my travelling, either for pleasure or health, I hope.
> Health now pretty good, as good probably as it will ever be.

Eliot's third and final journey to Europe, like the first, marked a time of decision for him. He returned from this trip in the spring of 1870, and on returning to St. Louis began a new volume of his journal. In it, on July 1, he noted that he had written and copied his letter of resignation as Pastor of the Church of the Messiah. He was 57 years old.

The reasons for this decision are not entirely clear. Since only a few months later he took up formally the responsibilities of Acting Chancellor of the University, it might be concluded that he resigned his pastorate in anticipation of concentrating his energies for this new vocation. However, it seems apparent that at the time of his resignation this was neither his anticipation nor wish.

Noting in his journal on September 8 that he had been an hour at the University, he commented:

> This new and presently exclusive work has no attractions for me. I may get used to it and mean to succeed. But it is a turn in my life which I take unwillingly: to return to my proper calling whenever I can.

There is no question as to what Eliot considered his proper calling, but except to the extent most people continued to think of him as the true Pastor of the Church of the Messiah even after the Installation of his successor in that role, he never returned to the ministry.

I believe Eliot submitted his resignation in 1870 simply because he felt it was time to do so. After 35 years he no longer felt adequate to its demands. Also, he had in mind a man whom he felt would be a suitable successor, a minister by the name of Woodbury.

In September, Eliot was formally appointed Acting Chancellor of the University, a role he had already been filling in fact though not in name. Chancellor Chauvenet had been seriously ill for some months. At a special meeting of the University Board of Trustees on February 21, while Eliot was still away, the resignation of Professor B. J. Tweed, who had been Acting Chancellor as well as Professor of English Literature, was accepted, and Professor A. Litton was requested to act as Chancellor "for the remainder of this term or until Dr. Eliot Pres. returns from Europe."

Thus 1870 is the year in which Eliot began the transition from his vocation as Pastor to that of educational administrator, from chancel to Chancellor. But the actual transition was more gradual and took place over several years. Even before 1870 Eliot had assumed many of the Chancellor's roles and responsibilities. And even after he was formally installed as the third Chancellor of the University in 1872, he continued his ministry.

Due, in Eliot's opinion at least, to the mishandling of the call by the church Trustees, when the invitation to Eliot's choice, Woodbury, was finally properly extended, it was declined. The unfortunate man ultimately chosen to be Eliot's successor in the pulpit was John Snyder, who was not installed until 1873, and until then Eliot continued as Pastor. Snyder never did succeed in getting out of the shadow of his illustrious predecessor.

Until Eliot's death in 1887 there was little question who the "real" pastor of the Church of the Messiah was. Even if Eliot had been more enthusiastic about his successor than he was, Snyder's role would have been a difficult one, and his pastorate, though long by today's standards, was undistinguished. Eliot did try to help. In 1876 he even offered to serve as Superintendent of the Sunday School, an act he intended to show his support of Snyder's ministry. On the other hand, when it came time to build a new church in 1879, it was Eliot who approved the site, at Locust and Garrison, chose the architects (Peabody and Stearns of Boston) and discretely oversaw the entire venture. There were two major addresses at the Dedication Service for the new Church of the Messiah, held on December 16, 1881. The first was the sermon by Henry Whitney Bellows of New York. The other was by Eliot, who also wrote a hymn for the occasion. Snyder, the only participant not listed in the program by name, but only as "The Pastor," after welcoming the congregation, sat and listened.

So the transition from chancel to Chancellor was gradual. Eliot's reluctance to accept what to many must have seemed the inevitability of his appointment as University Chancellor, a reluctance born of his consecration to the ministerial vocation, is probably the major reason why the transition had not taken place sooner. Even as Acting Chancellor, Eliot encouraged the Chancellorship Committee to find someone other than himself to fill the role permanently. The Chancellorship was endowed at this time, with a gift from Hudson E. Bridge, a church member and one of the Charter members of the University's Board of Directors, of $100,000 for this purpose, so money was not an obstacle in the search. The Chancellorship Committee's report in August of 1871 reflects both the difficulties they had encountered in interesting anyone else suitable for the role, and also their clear convictions on the matter. The report may be read as an argument addressed to the Acting Chancellor. It says in part:

> In view of the wants and necessities of the institution present as well as for some years to come we feel that the institution should have a head, and not an acting or nominal head, and we know of no one if he can be induced to accept the position, and sunder himself from all other alliances, who is so capable and so well suited as our present acting Chancellor. . . . [The University] is the child of his heart. . . . There is none other that can ever feel for and take the same interest in it, which he has done and will continue to do. . . .
>
> There is no person who we could likely induce to take charge of it that is so widely and favorably known, and who is so universally honored and esteemed. His reputation is a national one, and no one would have to ask who is the Chancellor of Washington University. He commands the esteem and respect as I am assured, of Professors, Tutors, and pupils. . . . While conservative in his views, he is still willing to acknowledge that the world moves and he moves with it. . . .

The report concluded with an invitation to Eliot to accept the Chancellorship at a salary of $5,000. It is an indication of the still precarious financial position of Washington University, despite all we shall hear about money in the remaining years of Eliot's life, that he never took any part of his salary. Salaries at Washington University during this period were hardly competitive with the Universities of the east. As one modern commentator has said: "To feel comfortable with his pay, a professor at Washington University had to regard his appointment there as something of a 'divine call' as did Eliot."

There seems to be more than polite modesty in Eliot's letter accepting the position of Chancellor in October of 1871:

> I regret very much the failure to find someone more suitable than myself to fill the place of Chancellor of Washington University, but . . . will accept . . . relying upon the judgement of the Directors . . . that the best interests of the University in all its Departments will thereby be promoted. For one or two years to come, it may perhaps be the best arrangement, and although I have been earnestly desirous of a different result, I shall do my best to justify the confidence now reposed in me.

Whatever actual inadequacies Eliot felt about himself, they did not prevent him from expressing confidence further along in this letter that the school "can be the leading University in the western valley *within five years.*" This high and hopeful expectation was typical, but was probably inspired in part by the success the University had recently been enjoying in its fund-raising efforts.

The burden of this effort had fallen mainly on Eliot from the beginning, and the generosity he elicited, particularly from some close associates and friends, is nothing short of extraordinary. Though the University was designedly non-sectarian, it was strongly associated with the Unitarian Church, and Eliot's early efforts to broaden its base of support — and potential benefactors — did not meet with much success. As he had done at the time of the building of the first church and during the Civil War in support of the Western Sanitary Commission, Eliot had again appealed to Unitarians in the east, particularly in Boston, in support of his new endeavor. In the spring of 1864 Eliot had come to Boston to present his case to the people there: of the $478,000 that had been contributed to Washington University, he told them, four-fifths had come from members of his own congregation, being for several years an annual average of $50,000. Eleven individuals had contributed $300,000 of this amount, among whom, he said, only two or three could be considered wealthy men. Several had given fifteen to thirty percent of their net worth, one had given sixty percent and had expressed willingness to give half the remainder.

Raising funds for the University became a constant preoccupation for the rest of Eliot's life. That his efforts were successful is suggested by some good-natured jests directed at him. A child swallowed a coin and a neighbor quipped: "Well, that's one dime Mr. Eliot won't get." A St. Louis businessman was widely though anonymously quoted as saying that if he could have had Dr. Eliot for a partner together they would have made most of the money west of the Alleghenies.

A Boston newspaper reported that "it has come to be an admitted fact that when Dr. Eliot announces that he must have so much money, either for Washington University, or a local mission, it is safe for the most prudent to make discount on this security."

And when A. A. Livermore, the President of Meadville Theological School, reported to the Unitarian National Conference on the status of several of the schools in which Unitarians had a major interest he concluded by saying that it seemed "a work of supererogation to advise any members of our communion of faith to make bequests to Washington University, for Dr. Eliot has but to lift his hand and strike his rod, and means and money flow in ever-gushing streams."

But in reality rather than hyperbole, the University's financial needs seemed to grow always a little faster than the available resources. From the beginning Eliot had envisioned a great university on a grand scale. He had told the people of Boston in 1864 that Washington University would become for the Mississippi Valley what Harvard was for New England. By 1870 the University had come much closer to this goal than anyone — including even Eliot himself — had thought it could in so short a time. Eliot was named Acting Chancellor on September 20, 1870. A few months later the University received gifts totaling $240,000, including $130,000 from Hudson E. Bridge, an amount which included the endowment for the Chancellorship mentioned earlier. Eliot wrote an exuberant letter to his son, enumerating the gifts and concluding: "This quite sets us up." Yet less than a year later upon his inauguration as Chancellor, Eliot called for a new fundraising goal. "Give us one million of dollars, and grant us five years' time, and we will provide for St. Louis and its region all the educational advantages of Harvard or Yale."

Arguing the necessity of these new funds to the Board of Directors Eliot said:
Gentlemen, I know that this persistent cry for money is wearisome in the extreme, but how can I help it when I see the greatness of the opportunity, the growing necessity of the work to be accomplished?

I doubt if there is a person in St. Louis who covets money or prays for it more earnestly than I do, and I feel an assured unreasoning conviction, "borne in upon me," that from one source or other the money will come. But I see it in such abundance around me, hoarded or wasted, that I scarcely know how patiently to wait for the comparatively small amount for the want of which our young university is compelled, like a child, to crawl and totter instead of vigorously marching on. One million of dollars, added to what we have, if properly invested, would secure to Washington University, in five years time and ever afterwards, a commanding influence throughout this great valley, and would go far toward making our city, what it cannot without some such agency become, the metropolis of the West.

We shall return at the end of this chapter to Eliot's inauguration as Chancellor in 1872, but our focus now is on the year 1870, in which he returned from Europe, submitted his resignation as Pastor of the Church of the Messiah and assumed the role of Acting Chancellor. Two other events mark the year. One was the death of his brother Thomas Dawes Eliot of New Bedford, Massachusetts, to whose death bed Eliot had come upon his return from Europe. He died on June 14. Thomas was a member of the United States Congress from Massachusetts; he was also the President of the National Conference of Unitarian Churches, the organization which had been established five years previously under the brilliant leadership of Henry Whitney Bellows of New York City. The National Conference represented the first true denominational form among the Unitarian churches, each of which was represented in the Conference by ministerial and lay delegates in a pattern not too dissimilar to that of the General Assembly of the present Unitarian Universalist Association.

From the beginning there was dissension over the theological basis of the Conference. The radicals opposed references to the Christian basis of Unitarianism and had succeeded, at the last of the biennial meetings of the Conference in 1868, in passing an amendment to the Constitution to their liking. This Amendment had been offered, actually as a kind of compromise move, by Eliot's old friend, James Freeman Clarke, but Eliot was not happy with it. He was not alone. The major point at issue at the Conference of 1870 was a motion to rescind the action taken two years before, a motion vigorously championed by Eliot. He had been invited to deliver the Conference Sermon, a highlight of each meeting which took place on the eve of the opening session, and it was perhaps inevitable that he would use this Sermon to support his position in the debate to follow.

But the Conference Sermon of 1870 became something much more for Eliot. It became a focal point for some of his deepest religious concerns, his fears about the directions he saw Unitarianism taking. It was also a kind of valedictory. He began work on it shortly after he had written his letter of resignation as Pastor of the Church of the Messiah. Although he did not actually relinquish the role for three more years the thought of leaving the ministry of the church was profoundly with him, as his notes for the Sermon, including long passages deleted in the final draft, indicate. From July on, the Notebooks show Eliot's preoccupation with the Conference Sermon. Scattered amid records of pastoral calls, lists of funds he was in the process of obtaining for the University's new scientific hall which he had announced in June, and references to sundry other activities, we find scattered notes and thoughts related to this one Sermon. The first of these notes indicates both some reluctance and a desire to re-frame the terms of the debate:

> I have promised to preach Conference sermon in N.Y. next Oct. 18; and am already half sorry. This is an important juncture in Religious affairs, and I am due to please nobody. Not only the division between Conservatives and Radicals, but now between those who wish a *Statement of Faith* or Quasi Creed, and those who do not — makes the matter intricate.

The theme of Eliot's sermon, which he titled "Christ and Liberty," was "The Gospel and the freedom of the Gospel." In his view religious freedom meant freedom from "1. Ritual Religion. 2. Superstitious fears. 3. Human control and Ecclesastiscism," including freedom from creeds, which were human forms. However, for him *"Perfect Freedom"* was also *"Perfect Allegiance* to Christ." It was perfect freedom, Eliot wrote in his early notes, because "His teachings are absolute truth" and "His commandments are the Law of God."

It may be difficult for us to understand today, because the language of the discussion has changed, but Eliot was trying to stake out a vital liberal middle ground between those who wanted a creed on the one hand and those who wanted to abandon the Christian basis of Unitarianism altogether on the other. One of his random notes says:

> "Unquestionably there may be another phase, Free Religion, outside of Chris-

tianity, but that would not be the Unitarian movement, and we cannot organize under it."

Another note, which found its way into the final version of the sermon, reads: "The distinctive work of the Unitarian body, its mission, has been to unite allegiance to Christ with intellectual freedom." From this mission, he argued, it was possible to depart in two different directions: "by adopting a creed — or symbol" or "by rejecting Christ as the Divine authority."

Interestingly, while he was opposed to the adoption of a church creed, his thinking about the subject apparently suggested to Eliot the idea of writing a personal creed, which we will discuss further in the final chapter.

Eliot's Conference Sermon of 1870 is one of the most passionate, eloquent and powerful of all his utterances. Had the cause of Unitarian Christianity which he championed ultimately prevailed, it would perhaps be one of the well-remembered documents and regarded as an historical milestone today. But he argued for a cause that was ultimately lost, and his words have been forgotten. Because of its importance, and as an example of Eliot's style, the complete text of this sermon has been included as an Appendix to this present volume. One of its most effective passages is remarkable not only for its eloquence but for its personal poignance. Seldom in a sermon did Eliot ever refer to himself; the rare occasions when he did so come forth with unusual power. In this case he was speaking directly from the depths of his heart as well as conviction:

> It is much easier to go away from the Christian religion than to improve upon it. I have sometimes thought, "so foolish was I and blind," that this is becoming the settled and determined tendency of our Unitarian body and of this Conference; that the banner upon which "Christ and Liberty" is inscribed is to be pulled down and another set up, on which liberty alone is written. Such thought, whenever it has come, has filled me with grief, for I love the Unitarian Church as I love my own family and home. But loyalty to Christ comes first. Speaking for myself, and I can speak only for myself, however dear to me the associations of the present and past, I could never consent to remain in any church or communion which is ashamed of Jesus Christ and his gospel. The act which strikes that name from the banner would strike my name from the role. The Christianity without Christ is no Christianity for me. With my convictions of duty I should have no right, and should feel no wish to be the member of any church, however refined and cultivated and liberal, where the name of Jesus Christ is held in doubtful honor, for I believe his words, "He that is ashamed of me, of him will I be ashamed."

"But thank God," he went on, "we have no abiding fear that that Unitarian body, or any part of it, will take such a suicidal course." Here he was speaking not from actual convictions but for homiletic effect; here he moved from personal testimony to political tactics. The practical purpose of his sermon, aside from the personal catharsis which it also clearly represented, was to lay the groundwork for the repeal of the radical's amendment of two years before. In this purpose he succeeded as the Amendment was overwhelmingly overturned by the Conference three days later, and the Christian basis of the Unitarian fellowship resoundingly reaffirmed. Ultimately, of course, this was a pyrrhic victory — and the denomination has since moved extremely far in the direction Eliot feared — but for the moment and for his lifetime the victory was won.

To his journal he confided:

"Well, my bothersome sermon is over. Conceived, born, delivered . . . One thing at any rate I have done. I have found my own soul. If I cannot stay in a church with as much a creed as I expressed — Christ first and Liberty afterwards — I am adrift."

1870 also marked the beginning of another concern which occupied much of Eliot's time and energy over the next few years. This concerned what in the polite euphemism of the times was called "the social evil." In St. Louis as well as other cities the licensing of prostitution was being proposed as a public health measure. Alongside the first newspaper article on this subject which Eliot posted in his journal, an article describing the regulations relative to this measure, Eliot noted, "This is a fearful experiment." Then he added, "If amended so as to register the *men* who visit, it would be a radical measure."

A few weeks later in a letter to the editor, Eliot spelled out his proposal in detail. Since the supposed purpose of the social evil legislation was the detection and prevention of disease, the male customers should be registered as well as the female prostitute, he said. "Let that registry be open to the police and examining physicians under such regulations and with such rights of inquiry as may tend to prevent the dissemination of disease. . ."

"I understand the objections which will be made to this," Eliot went on. "But such objections are founded upon a one-sided justice. Men are the lawmakers, and wish for an immunity in wrong doing and an exemption from penalties which they will not allow women. I say that so far as possible, all should be treated alike. . . . Any man who visits a house of ill fame and approves the law as it now is, but condemns a legislation that would reach himself, is open to the charge of being a tyrant and a hypocrite."

Of course the actual effect of such a change, as Eliot well knew, would be the repeal of the social evil legislation altogether, an object which Eliot worked toward and which was successfully achieved in a few months. "We can never put down vice by giving it the sanction of law," he wrote.

But if in 1870 Eliot reveals his conservatism in his religious views, and his Puritanism in his views on the social evil, he reveals his liberal and in the time perhaps even radical side, in his views regarding women's rights, though it should always be remembered that Eliot thought less in terms of rights than of responsibilities, less of opportunities than obligations, less of privileges than of duty.

On the 16th of October Eliot noted in his journal that to his surprise, "*all* the Faculty . . . were in favor of admitting young women into college classes either for special recitations or as full students." This was pleasing to Eliot, who strongly favored the decision.

Although he later confessed that he "came slowly and almost reluctantly to the position," in general Eliot seems to have been relatively advanced in his views on women's rights. During the later part of 1870 he prepared, and in December delivered, a lecture on "Women's Work in America, and the Education Needed to Prepare them for It."

The 19th Amendment granting women the right to vote would not be passed for another 49 years, but Eliot said that women's suffrage was inevitable and used it to advance his case for the general availability of educational opportunity for women.

This is one of the most modern-sounding of all Eliot's writings:

> Our reading of history leads us to see, in the records both of ancient and modern civilizations, that although there has been a great deal of generosity in the treatment of women, there has been very little justice. There has been chivalry and worship, but little confidence and respect. Protection has been vouchsafed her, but never the right to protect herself. But without such right, no class in society can be safe. Power is the only principle which society permanently respects. In a monarchy or aristocracy, the common people are sure to be oppressed and their rights invaded. In a republic, an unrepresented class is the sure victim of injustice. The ballot box and equal representation is the only way to secure equality of rights.
>
> In my judgement, therefore, it is [only] a question of time when the ballot shall stand among women's conceded rights. . . . Upon the certainty of their

extended rights of citizenship — and this is the point here to be made — the education of young women should be shaped.

Near the conclusion of these remarks which were given as part of the program of the Missouri State Teacher's Association held at Sedalia, December 27–29, Eliot said:

What then will come of all this, do you say? Are we to have women doctors, and lawyers, and clergymen, and civil engineers, and public officers until men are pushed out of their places and the whole order of society is deranged? We answer, that under the providential ordering of human relations and interests such questions may be left to themselves. For a time foolish women will do foolish things and hundreds will undertake what they cannot perform. But the laws of social science, of experience, of sound political economy, will gradually set things right, and in every department of work those who by natural capacity and education are best fitted for the work to be done, and, by mental and physical constitution are best able to perform it, whether men or women, will soon find that they have it to do.

So this was the year, 1870. Not all of it, to be sure, but I hope that I have succeeded in my goal to give an impression of the kind and variety of endeavor which occupied Eliot in this time near the height of his achievement and his fame. I shall conclude by quoting at some length from the remarks delivered by Mr. Wayman Crow at the formal Installation of Dr. Eliot as Third Chancellor of Washington University, on February 29, 1872, a date which formally marks his taking up the position which he would so honorably fill for the next fifteen years and the beginning of the last chapter of Eliot's life:

Mr. Crow, on behalf of the board of directors, delivered to him the charter of the university, as a symbol of the power conveyed to him, and in addressing him said in part: "More than thirty years ago, when St. Louis was little more than a frontier village, you first became intimately connected with the educational interests of this city as director and subsequently president of the public school board, and we do not forget that it was owing in a great part to your efforts, and to the earnest cooperation of those who were associated with you in those early days, that we are indebted for the admirable system of common schools which we now possess, and for the preservation of the liberal endowment, which, in the space of a single lifetime, has enabled it to attain a degree of excellence and bring forth fruits that may safely challenge comparison. . . . From the moment when with fear and hope it was first decided to give a practical shape and form to the idea of this institution, down to the present occasion, when in the full tide of successful experiment we call you to the highest and most responsible of academic positions, the burthen of the labor has rested on your shoulders; as president of the board of directors, it fell within your province to prepare and develop the general plan upon which the success of the experiment was believed to depend; to you was committed the duty of organizing the different departments of instruction as they were rendered necessary to accommodate the ever widening circle of scholars; and at the same time you have not only had the entire supervision of the material interests of the institution, but you voluntarily assumed the task of placing its affairs upon such a basis, which I trust will soon be accomplished, as to make them comparatively independent of financial change and vicissitude. All these results have been attained, and that Washington University exists today, with its doors wide open and hundreds of scholars thronging its halls, is due to your energy, executive ability, and unselfish devotion to the sacred cause of education. Do not be surprised, therefore, if we salute you as its 'founder,' for in so doing we but echo the unanimous sentiments of those who have shared your anxieties, participated however humbly in your labors, and who now rejoice in the glorious prospect of success."

MISCELLANY, 1872–1880

Excerpts from Eliot's Inaugural Address, upon his formal Installation as Chancellor of Washington University on February 29, 1872:

"We recognize the duty of an American University to address itself to the everyday working world of a republic where every man is a sovereign, by opening its doors as wide as possible to everyone, male or female, who can find time and disposition, if it be but for a few hours a week in the long winter evenings, or by occasional consultation with competent teachers appointed for the purpose. Thus, the best educated mind of the university world should be brought into immediate contact with the practical organization of the working world, to the advantage of both. Thus, the conventional wall of separation between working men of the hand and working men of the head may be thrown down. The fancied preeminence of the learned professions would disappear. A good education would gradually come to be recognized as a necessity in the training of every young man, whether for intellectual or mechanical pursuits. We believe this is not the age or country, certainly not in this valley of the West, for the great activities of intellectual culture to keep aloof from the common mind. The University should be the leaven to act with creative and purifying power until the whole mass is leavened. Such has been and is our aim."

*   *   *

"Not quantity but quality of work is the ultimate test of a university's success. To educate one man thoroughly, to carry him above the standard of his times, to make him one of those who stand first, leading, not following the world's movements, confers more honor than to graduate a thousand upon the usual dead level of moderate scholarship. Nay, in this respect and rightly considered, quality of results includes quantity, and one man educated to do first-rate work weighs more and counts more than many who are only competent to deal in second-hand ideas and to follow beaten tracks. One best is more than many good. The man who looks a little further than his contemporaries discovers a new continent. The man who thinks a little more profoundly, invents the telegraph or reveals the laws of light. To train one such man, or to clear his way before him, adds more to the world's wealth, and gives greater impetus to the world's civilization than numerical figures can compute.

"Therefore it is, that the University should be supplied with all needful facilities for giving the best education to the few, as well as a good education to the many. The number may be small of those who are by nature capable of receiving the best gifts, but the best gifts should be kept ready, and no one, honestly seeking for them, should be turned away."

*   *   *

"Washington University, in its ante-typal idea, prefigures an Institution worthy of the great name it bears: a name which is the symbol of Christian civilization and American patriotism, and to which, therefore, no thought of sectarian narrowness or of party strife can ever be attached; an Institution of learning, at once conservative and progressive, with foundations so broad that there is room for every department of human culture, and so deep that neither praise nor blame shall shake its allegiance to truth."

*   *   *

"There is no such word as fail. There is no such word. In our moral dictionaries it has no place and we will not admit it there."

*   *   *

"Shall we succeed? Shall we see the work prosper in our hands? I think, I believe, I feel assured that many of us will. Yet let us never forget that there's a divinity that shapes our ends, rough hew them as we will.

"Expect the Lord build the house — except the Lord build the University — they labor in vain that bless it."

*   *   *

"Spring begins to come. Less than two months to "vacation," the first I have ever had as a right.

"If we could only get a good living pastor I should be reconciled, partially, to the new vocation."

— WGE, Notebook entry, April, 1872

*   *   *

Excerpts from Eliot's speech on the occasion of Washington University's 25th Anniversary:

"They who come nearest to truth come nearest to God, and whoever puts hindrance in the way, with however good intention, should take heed lest haply he be found to be fighting against Him."

*   *   *

"Science and philosophy are by their nature conservative [and] they are sure to come back again with the prodigal's humility to the Father's house. Give to truth the fair and open field of freedom, and the ultimate conquest over falsehood and error may be held as the certain result. Truth fears nothing but concealment. Let the motto of our University be, 'Veritas pro veritate' — Truth for truth's sake."

*   *   *

"One purpose of an endowed institution is to furnish the best education at low rates, so as to keep a certain hospitality to all comers. It is a serious evil in a republic to draw a strong line between rich and poor, and to exclude from the best schools all who are of restricted income."

*   *   *

"It is a very poor reputation which cannot afford to be misunderstood."

— WGE to H. W. Barber, July 28, 1879

*   *   *

"Shall you be at Saratoga [for the meeting of the National Unitarian Conference]? . . . Is there any hope of a New Departure, by making the Gospel of Work and of high personal morality take the place of speculation and denial? Unless we can accomplish that, with all our learning, the reason for our denomination's existence will soon cease. To preach to the Educated classes, the men of science, the women of thought and wisdom, the leaders of society, the Educators of the people, Repentance and good works, self-denial and self-consecration, in the service of God (the great task-master's eye) — is our mission, if we have any — a work harder than that of Wesley or Fox, but equally demanded."

— WGE to James Freeman Clarke, August 22, 1880

*   *   *

Third church building, Northeast corner of Garrison and Locust
Dedicated December 16, 1881
(Courtesy First Unitarian Church Archives)

CHAPTER VI
"LOOKING UNTO JESUS"

"We can do all things through Christ, nothing without him."

William Greenleaf Eliot spent the last summer of his life, 1886, in Jefferson, New Hampshire, a beautiful area of the White Mountains where he had often vacationed before. While there he celebrated his 76th and last birthday on August 5, and on that day wrote a poem, "Nunc Dimittis." The poem reflects weariness and weakness, his welcoming acceptance of death, yet ends with a typical remonstrance to himself, that as long as the task of life is unfinished, as long as one lives, the call to work and duty must prevail. The Latin title of the poem refers to the gospel passage which begins, "Lord, now lettest thou thy servant depart in peace, according to thy word: For mine eyes have seen thy salvation, which thou hast prepared before the face of all people, a light to lighten the Gentiles, and the glory of thy people Israel."

"Nunc Dimittis"

Fain would I breathe that gracious word,
Now lettest thou thy servant, Lord,
   Depart in peace.
When may I humbly claim that kind award,
   And cares and labors cease?
With anxious heart I watch at heaven's gate —
   Answer to hear;
With failing strength I feel the increasing weight
   Of every passing year.
Hath not the time yet fully come, dear Lord,
   Thy servant to release?

Be still, my heart! In silence God doth speak,
Here is thy place; here, not at heaven's gate;
Thy task is not yet finished; frail and weak,
Doing or suffering, steadfast in thy faith,

> Thy service is accepted, small or great;
> His time is thine — or soon or late,
> If daylight fades, work while the twilight lasts.

The twilight lasted only a few months more. Returned to St. Louis in the fall, in steadily declining health, he was taken to Pass Christian, Mississippi, at the beginning of the New Year for the milder climate, and in this appropriately named place, William Greenleaf Eliot died on January 23, 1887.

His body was immediately returned to St. Louis, and on January 27, funeral services were held. Eliot had written a list of instructions regarding arrangements after his death: "Let my funeral be very quiet, without show or parade of any kind. Better if the assembled friends be dismissed and my family, with needful assistance only, follow my coffin to the grave." Two of his sons, the Reverend Thomas Lamb Eliot of Portland, Oregon, and the Rev. Christopher Rhodes Eliot of Boston, conducted family services before the public ceremony at the Church of the Messiah on Locust and Garrison, which was filled to overflowing for the occasion. Following Eliot's instruction, no eulogy was delivered. The service consisted mainly of music and readings from scripture, after the pattern Eliot had set down in the church's *Prayer Book* many years before.

The procession from the Church to Bellefontaine Cemetery was not the family only, as Eliot had envisioned, but virtually the entire civic leadership of the City of St. Louis, the University, the public schools, and hundreds of others — both parishioners and not — who had been touched by his life. The newspapers noted that all eight pall-bearers were men — not of his own family — who had been named for Dr. Eliot: Eliot H. Chamberlain, Hudson Eliot Bridge, Eliot Jewett, Eliot Todd, William Eliot Smith, Eliot Collender, William Eliot Ware, and William Eliot Furness. Eliot's grave at Bellefontaine Cemetery was marked with a small stone, on which following his request was inscribed only his name, dates of birth and death, and the three words, "Looking Unto Jesus." Thus was buried the man who had written to his best friend while still contemplating his decision to move to St. Louis in 1834: "If I come, I come to remain, and to lay my ashes in the valley of the Mississippi."

On the day of his funeral, a short article on the front page of the weekly Unitarian newspaper, *The Christian Register,* published in Boston, appeared:

> The telegraph brings the news of the death of Rev. William Greenleaf Eliot, D.D., of St. Louis. . . . His death recalls the history of a noble life spent in the service of humanity. . . . As Starr King is inseparably connected with the history of California, so Dr. Eliot is inseparably connected with the history of Missouri. There is not a bell in the State that ought not to toll in his memory.

The following week's issue of the *Register* included lengthy articles on Eliot, including a reprint from the St. Louis papers published on the day of his death, which asserted that for fifty years Eliot had been associated with "all that is best in St. Louis," and emphasized Eliot's personal character. "In preaching," it said, "he had few equals."

> But it was the daily beauty of his life which chiefly influenced those to whom he spoke. . . . Reference has been made to the work [Washington University] which will be his monument; but the expression is misleading, for it seems to imply that he will be remembered, only, or chiefly by reason of some one achievement, and nothing can be more unjust. His life's work is the best part of the civil history of St. Louis for the last half-century.

Referring to Eliot's "characteristic objection" to the naming of the newly-chartered School, Eliot Seminary, after himself, this article noted: "It was his peculiarity to efface himself; to do his work — or as he called it, his Master's work — but not to glorify himself."

In the weeks and months following Eliot was remembered and honored in the pulpit and in the press throughout the country. In a sermon at King's Chapel, Boston, Henry W. Foote paid lengthy tribute:

> To thousands of people all over this country, Dr. Eliot is St. Louis and St. Louis means simply Dr. Eliot. If the greatness of a man's work is to be measured not by the noise which he may make for a little space, but by the extent to which he impressed himself upon a whole community, and shaped its institutions and enlarged and deepened its true life, then our time has seen few as great as he.

In Chicago, Joseph Shippen, *Esq.*, paid tribute to Eliot in a speech which unfortunately contained a number of errors of fact, but was strong in praise and in patriotism:

> Even as Dr. Bellows in the East, and Starr King on the Pacific coast, by tongue and pen inspired at home patriotic love of Union, and voluntary contributions to save and prevent suffering in the field, so did Dr. Eliot devote his energies to the same cause in the Mississippi Valley, and with like grandly successful results.

Perhaps the best and most extensive of these memorial tributes was written by a colleague and friend, the Rev. John H. Heywood, of Cincinnati, who had known Eliot for nearly 50 years. Heywood captured in a few sentences that, even though infected to some degree by a preacher's hyperbole, summarize as perhaps only a friend could, some of the main features of Eliot's ministry and character:

> No man knew better than Dr. Eliot how to find work for people to do, and how to set people on doing it. His mind — of rare clearness of vision, and with fixedness of purpose and executive power as rare — was ruled by the two great ideas of stewardship and consecration. Time, talent, money, opportunity, power of influence — all were trusts for which he and his people were to give strict account. . . .
>
> Wonderful, indeed — in some instances seeming almost miraculous — was [his] influence. There were in that early congregation men of large souls, generous by nature, who were instantly and always ready to respond to his appeals. Others there were, upright and honest, who, by constitutional bias or inherited tendency, found keeping much easier than giving; who, in fact, found giving very hard; and who, in other circumstances, under other influences, could readily have developed into "poor rich men," but who, through his teaching and illustrative example, and with a growing sense of stewardship, became large and constant givers, upon whose intelligent and generous cooperation, whenever important work was to be done — work calling for free exercise of the self-denying spirit — he could rely with absolute confidence. . . .
>
> In such ways was the church trained and educated. Its minister constantly expected great things, and the people responded to his expectations.

So even in a progressive era characterized by optimism and hopefulness, and in a place — the west — which symbolized the growth and expansion of the nation, Eliot was notable for the high level of his expectations. "The past has much for which we may be reasonably grateful," he told the members of the Church of the Messiah gathered to celebrate the church's 50th Anniversary, "but the future must and will have greater things in store."

This attitude of high hopefulness, of great expectations, is the first of several traits which seem most significant in evaluating the life and character of William Greenleaf Eliot. Having now traced some of the details of his life, it remains to enumerate some of these facets of his character.

High on this list, and not unconnected to his attitude of high expectations, was a deeply rooted sense of morality and a belief in the pre-eminent importance of moral education. The lengthy memorial tribute to Eliot adopted by the Washington University Trustees three days after his death concluded with these sentences:

> In the administration of this institution his ideals of intellectual culture, always high, kept well advanced the moral aspect of education in the development of

character; and he deemed no system of education complete which did not look to Christian manhood and womanhood as the end to be attained.

The formation of Christian character was, for Eliot, the ultimate end and objective of anything worthy of being called education. By "Christian character" Eliot meant nothing sectarian, but he did mean something specific. He was essentially a Puritan moralist. He believed in the ultimate perfection of society through the gradual perfection of individuals who compose a society. True moral progress was achieved only from the inside out. A better society could only be obtained by the moral development of individuals — and individual moral progress depended upon the right education of body, mind and spirit.

Thus, anything destructive of mind, body or spirit was regarded as evil, and something destructive to all three, such as alcohol, was an evil of an extreme degree. For the Puritan it was a given that the law existed chiefly to serve moral purposes. As education could support moral progress, legislation could at least limit its decline. Although the fact is not widely noted today, temperance was one of the major social reforms forwarded by Unitarians in the 19th century, Eliot prominently among them. In his later years he bewailed the waning enthusiasm among Unitarians for the temperance cause. Alcohol, he thought, was the single major source of both personal misery and social disruption. In a letter written a year before his death to his son Christopher, who carried on his father's work in this area, Eliot noted that the churches had at one time been as tender-footed on the slavery issue as he now felt them to be on temperance. Denouncing the liquor traffic in absolute terms, in this letter he declared it "a hundred times more destructive of society, body and soul, than slavery in its worst days."

Similar passion animated Eliot's opposition to the so-called "Social Evil" legislation, which provided for the licensing of prostitutes and prostitution, and — in effect — legalized prostitution in St. Louis. The law was passed by the city council on July 5, 1870, but it was not until 1873 that Eliot was ready to lead a full-scale assault through the courts and the newspapers, resulting in its nullification early in 1874. After this, Eliot actively supported those working against similar legislation in other cities.

Corresponding to these negative efforts to attack vice were those positive efforts, plainly more congenial to Eliot personally, to establish and build up those institutions and enterprises, churches and schools chief among them, which have as their goal personal moral elevation — or as Eliot put it, the education of Christian character. Eliot was pre-eminently an institution-builder. Not necessarily, as he had confessed to.Margaret Fuller so many years before, a creatively original thinker, he possessed in great measure the capacity to cast others' ideas into useful forms, into organizations and institutions of public service. But he was no mere "organization man." The purpose of each enterprise was more important than its form. Institutions which were dedicated to uplifting individuals — in body, mind, or spirit — were, he believed, the major instrument of the improvement of society, both the means and certain sign of permanent progress. Thus the permanence of such institutions was in certain respects even more important than their initial establishment. For their significance in part was to embody and symbolize the commitment of the community to constant individual improvement and thus of social progress.

All of these are not merely philosophical points but clues to Eliot's character: an attitude of great expectations, a strong moral sense, and a belief in social progress through the moral development of individuals — all combined with a capacity to build institutions designed to promote such progress in individuals to the lasting benefit of society at large. But one key element is missing from this list, the element of faith.

Eliot lived a life of religious passion. In body physically weak, even frail, his life illustrates the reality and the dominance of spiritual strength and energy. "We can do all things through Christ, nothing without him," he wrote. Whether true universally or of anyone else, it was unquestionably true for him. He was engaged in a high and holy purpose, his Master's work. We cannot understand Eliot at all without a deep understanding of this element of his character, allegiance to Christ.

As early as 1840, about six years after his arrival in St. Louis, Eliot had indicated that his religious beliefs were becoming more traditional since his settlement in the west. To his friend and seminary schoolmate, James Freeman Clark, he wrote in November of that year: "I am more Orthodox than when we knew each other, and still going in that direction. I bind myself more and more to Jesus Christ, and accord him more and more authority and honor."

By the end of his life the Unitarian denomination had drifted from its exclusively Christian foundations, a tendency which Eliot adamantly opposed and deplored, as we have seen. In 1870 he went so far as to draft and have printed what he called "A Confession of Unitarian Christian Faith." Though this was a personal statement, and Eliot never thought of proposing it for adoption by any church, it was widely distributed in St. Louis and at least a few other places. A Portland, Oregon, newspaper printed it as being representative of Unitarianism in that city, where the Unitarian Church of Our Father was pastored by Eliot's oldest son, Thomas. It was probably widely distributed among the more conservative Unitarians:

I believe in One God the Father Almighty, Maker of Heaven and earth, who is the Only True God, above all and through all and in us all; and in one Lord Jesus Christ, His beloved Son, our Savior, who came from God to bear witness to the truth, as one having authority; to do the perfect will of the Father; to suffer and die, the just for the unjust, and to rise again from the dead, according to the Scripture, that he might save his people from their sins, and reconcile the world to God.

I believe in the saving and sanctifying influences of the Holy Spirit of God, working in us both to will and to do, of his good pleasure; in the forgiveness of sin and the Gospel of Eternal life; in the necessity of repentance and regeneration; in the sinfulness of all mankind; in the just retribution of sin, both in this world and the world to come; and in the final reconciliation of all things to God.

I believe in the Holy Scriptures, as the record of God's revelations to men and the sufficient rule of faith and practice; in the Christian Church, numbering, under whatever name, all sincere followers of Jesus Christ; in the universal brotherhood of man; in the Christian law, to do to others as we would that they should do to us; in the direct responsibility of every one to God; and in the right and duty of private judgment.

Eliot composed this "confession" on September 11, 1870. Nine days later he was officially named Acting Chancellor of Washington University. From this time until his death 17 years later, he served as Chancellor while not relinquishing the role of President of the Board which he had held since the school's founding. In this dual role he held ultimate responsibility for both the educational/philosophical and financial/institutional concerns of the institution. The University was expanding, both in programs already established and by the addition of new departments. Eliot was even more relentless as an educational innovator than as a fundraiser, it seems, or in any case there was always need of a little more money than was presently available.

But the University was far from his sole concern during these final years of his life. He wrote lengthy articles, as well as innumerable short newspaper pieces and letters, on such subjects as Temperance and the Social Evil Legislation. He published his one purely secular book, a biography of a slave he had helped to free by the name of Archer Alexander, and he oversaw new editions of some of his older books, mostly collections of sermons and lectures. He took up the cause of women's rights, an issue on which he was quite progressive. He wrote a couple of rather chiding letters to his old friend Clarke suggesting a lack of zeal on Clarke's part on behalf of women's suffrage in Massachusetts. I suspect that Eliot, who was generally more conservative than his friend on both social and religious issues, rather enjoyed this opportunity to turn the tables on him a bit.

But more than all the issues and concerns that involved him throughout his life, above even the University which was indeed the "child of his heart" and the focus of so much of his energy, there was a greater devotion which he never forgot. His work in the world was part of his duty to God, following the example of Christ.

It will be remembered that Eliot was Ordained as an Evangelist in the church of William Ellery Channing. Channing, the founder of American Unitarianism, had married Eliot's parents. Eliot was not only the progenitor of what became the single most important family in American Unitarian history, but was also himself a branch from the deeper roots of that history in his Puritan ancestry. American Unitarianism is more directly a child of Calvin than of Servetus. While the Unitarian Controversy resulted in a split in the New England Puritan churches along doctrinal lines, there was continuity with the older tradition on both sides. Trinitarians *and* Unitarians both claimed to best represent Christian faith. Channing himself opposed denominationalism; he wished Unitarianism never to become a separate sect. To Channing and to Eliot Christianity was simple, pure, religion, as it had first been preached by Jesus, and according to this view Unitarianism sought to restore Christianity in its purity and simplicity.

Eliot attributed to his contemporary, the English Unitarian theologian James Martineau, the notion of radical conservatism. The radical conservative drives the roots deeper, Eliot argued; and the deepest roots of Christianity were not in the creeds, not in the practices of the early church, but in the character and teaching of Jesus, of which Eliot believed the gospels give a true account. Eliot's personal, family and religious history are rooted in the Jesus of this tradition. It was as a disciple, one attempting to follow the example of that life and that teaching to which Eliot referred when he spoke of doing his Master's work.

One of the most intriguing of Eliot's ideas is what we may call "The Practical Argument for Christianity." Eliot was an eminently practical man. His personal faith was deeply-rooted and unquestionably sincere, but he also understood Christianity in utilitarian terms. Christianity was the practical means available that was most likely to accomplish the civilizing effects, the moral elevation of individuals and society, which were needed in the west. Eliot wore proudly the label of Christian Evangelist; this he felt was his true vocation: the establishment of Christian institutions and the development of Christian character in the west.

Not in the least does this suggest that Eliot was a cynical pragmatist. He could not have "used" Christianity had he not believed in it heart and soul. Faith must be the ground and inspiration for works, and the deeper and more passionate the faith, the greater will be the result flowing from it. And so what Eliot feared most in the growing latitudinarianism among the Unitarians was its tendency to foster a luke-warm faith, both in the laity and among ministers. His appeals to Boston for additional missionaries — ministers in the west — always stressed the need for zealous, faith-filled men. He wrote:

> It is sometimes thought that the way to reach worldly men, and to commend our [Unitarian] preaching is to meet them half-way; to preach doctrines that do not require too much faith, and are not strict enough to arouse their fears. No blunder could be greater than that. . . . Irreligious men are not attracted by skepticisms

and denials, but rather amused or disgusted. In the midst of their sins and neglect of God, they have sense enough to know that the fault is not in Christ's gospel but in their own waywardness and guilt. If they come to the religious life at all, they ask for a Saviour in whom they can trust.

Addressing younger ministers directly, he said:

Compare your actual success with that of men not half as strong in education and knowledge as yourselves. Why are they doing twice as much work? Because they work with stronger and more definite faith. They have an authority to lean upon to which you dare not appeal. There is no use in your going forth as missionaries unless you have a positive and clearly defined religion to teach. . . . Especially in the stirring and practical West, youthful lucubrations and Hegelian researches are not what men go to church to hear. They want plain preaching, founded upon the word of God.

"Why can we not use a little logic and common-sense in religious as well as secular affairs?" Eliot asked. It was a practical, common-sensical point to him when he said, "It is much easier to go away from the Christian religion than to improve upon it."

The distinctive Unitarian work, Eliot believed, was to maximize individual freedom of belief, but for him this was entirely consistent with what he understood to be the essentials of Christian faith. This was because gospel truth was not different or separate from truth. Logic and faith both pointed to the same conclusion.

In his most developed argument of this point, Eliot acknowledges that the philosophical way to truth is equal intellectually with the Christian way. His argument for the superiority of the Christian way is, again, a practical one:

There are two conceivable ways by which men may come to the knowledge of the highest spiritual truth and to a perfect system of morality. One may be called, for distinction, the rational or philosophical; the other is the path of Christian obedience. By the former a few persons of studious minds and with opportunity for self-scrutiny and metaphysical thought may rise from step to step, seeking after God if haply they may find Him, until at last they come to the highest that man can know, and find it to be the same which Jesus taught to the Samaritan woman eighteen hundred years ago: "God is a Spirit, and they that worship Him must worship Him in spirit and in truth." Or, in seeking to attain the perfect ideal of human virtue, we determine to live every day up to our highest convictions of duty, to do no wrong, to indulge no impure thought, to have no selfish motive, to make the best of every faculty, and control every tendency of evil. Slowly and painfully we struggle upwards, with many doubts and fears, questioning of the way and with uncertain aim, until, having labored long and hard, we come, perhaps to one who "opens the Scriptures," and shows us, in Christ's example and the gospel system of morality, the rule by which we have unwittingly been striving to live.

Eliot's point, and his conviction was that rationality and religion, philosophy and Christianity, both lead to the same place. Gospel truth is simply truth. Christian revelation is simply the revelation of the nature of things, of the way things are. The alternatives, as he believed, are not between two differing truths, but between two different paths to the one truth: the one, the rational or philosophical way, the other, the path of Christian obedience. Next he says:

To the vast majority of men, and to the young universally, the plainer path of Christian obedience is the safer way. Others may judge for themselves; but for myself I am ready to avow my need of a guide and Saviour.

Eliot does not argue that the path of Christian obedience is better, or faster, or easier than the philosophical way — he says it is safer, meaning that a person following this path, particularly a young person, is less likely to be led astray. This is partly out of a moral concern, but overall Eliot makes basically a practical argument for the Christian way: on the personal level, the gospel works.

He made much the same, practical argument on the institutional level as well:

> All over the Western States, where the call for Liberal Christianity has so often been heard, little bands of earnest men and women have gathered, with every hope of success, and for a time the cause of Christ and liberty has promised well, but too often it has ended in dullness and decay and death. . . . And why? Because neither gospel preaching nor Christian institutions have been the agency employed. Dispensing with the Christian ordinances, with prayer-meetings and Bible instructions to the young, speaking of Jesus Christ as seldom as possible, and never, by any chance, calling Him Lord or Master, the pulpit has sunk into insignificance and the pews into emptiness.

Late in his life, in correspondence, Eliot emphasized that he had no objection to the non-Christian, philosophical/rational approach *per se* — which is consistent with his belief that ultimately it reaches the same truths as the Christian path — but felt that it should not masquerade under the Unitarian name. To a colleague in 1885, he wrote:

> Let us stand for what we are. If we have outgrown Jesus Christ, let us openly avow it, as we have a right to do; but we have not the right, in that case, to hold to the name "Unitarian," which implies and always has implied "Christian."

Several months later, he wrote to his son, Christopher, expressing similar thoughts and confidence that the word Unitarian could be "redeemed to its historical meaning:"

> A "Unitarian Church" which rejects belief in God, in Christ, in Immortality, is a falsehood, a lie. As an Ethical Society I could work with it and honor it; but first change its name.

And in another letter to Christopher, written near the end of his life, he again emphasized his belief that the way of Christ and the way of truth are one and the same:

> Whatever has been successful in my 52 years of service, of whatever kind, comes from one principle, "looking unto Jesus." Truth for Truth's sake, in God's name; but the highest stretch of liberty, the most faithful development of my ideal of truth and righteousness, thus far, only brings me nearer to Him. To separate our churches from his spiritual guidance, would be cutting branches from the vine.

Eliot continued to preach during the later years of his life. Many of these sermons were for ceremonial or special occasions. But other than these his sermons dwelt almost entirely upon one theme. In September of 1885, when he was preaching regularly again at the Church of the Messiah during Snyder's temporary absence, he wrote in his journal:

> Somehow I feel like preaching but one word, as if I were a parrot, Jesus Christ. That is the one lesson to learn. To be ashamed of him is to bury all religion, all hope, all grandness of life's purpose. Allegiance to him, as the grand moral teacher, is the one essential to moral and philosophic success.

This same entry also stressed the theme that there was no conflict between science and Christianity, "for the truth of things and the truth of ideas cannot be in conflict."

This present work cannot more appropriately conclude than with an excerpt from what is believed to be Eliot's last written sermon. Entitled "The Personal Faith of Jesus" and delivered first on March 8, 1885, in St. Louis, in it Eliot developed four beliefs which he said were essential to the religion of Jesus of Nazareth, another way for him to speak of the essentials of Christianity: Faith in

God, Faith in Immortality, Faith in Universal Brotherhood, and Faith in his own Divine Mission.

It is the last of these beliefs — Faith in his own Divine Mission — which is not only the heart of this sermon, but contains the key to Eliot's entire life: duty and work in the service of God after the example of Christ.

Finally, if we would fully enter into these great truths to make them practically our own, we must according to our measure apply to ourselves, individually, the last named of his personal beliefs.

Recognizing the wide difference between ourselves and him, our spiritual guide, our redeemer, the chief among many brethren, yet in common with him we may reverently claim a mission from God, a work given us to do; a mission that we must fulfill, a work which, individually in our several places, we must finish if we want to die at peace with ourselves.

What that work may be is comparatively of no importance. To a great degree it is providentially determined. It may be much or little, but the widow's mite may be more in the final estimate than the rich man's abundance. "Act *well* thy part, there all the honor lies."

To the young therefore we say — both to young men and maidens — have some fixed aim in life. Let daily self-improvement, by the discipline of mind and character, and daily usefulness be your steadfast purposes. Now, in the days of youthful enjoyment and hope, let your service of God begin. The whole of your mortal life is not too great an offering to God. You cannot begin the work of self-consecrating devotion to duty too soon. Make your life worth living from the first. Let no wild oats be sown, for be well assured a day of reaping will come. Your sin will, sooner or later, find you out.

To those who are in the mature years of active and responsible life, their own experience brings the lesson of wisdom. Work diligently while it is day. No man can *serve* God and mammon — one or the other must be the master. As cares accumulate and the conflict of interests becomes fierce, possess your souls in patience and go no faster and no further than a scrupulous conscience will approve. Do your work in the world and at home faithfully and make it from first to last a practical fulfillment of the law of Christ. Let the religious element, a conscious responsibility to God, pervade all your work and all your enjoyments and all your defeats. Thus will the highest success of intelligent endeavor be attained.

And for us who stand at the limit of the appointed years, or already beyond it, let us remember that while there is life there is work to do. Put not off the armor of battle until the battle is over and the victory won. The closing years of a faithful life-service are oftentimes the best. By a true spirit of self-sacrifice now, we may add force and strength to all that has gone before. The extended years need not to be "of labor and sorrow." They may possess more than youthful vigor, as the service of time is passing into the service of eternity.

Thus, with our hearts full of the faith by which the Lord Jesus was himself perfected, we may all labor with him for our own salvation and for the regeneration of the world, until the appointed time comes, whether in youth or mature years or old age, when we can thankfully say, "I have finished the work Thou gavest me to do." *Amen.*

William Greenleaf Eliot circa 1885
(Courtesy Washington University Archives)

APPENDIX A

Excerpts from a letter by Abby Adams Cranch Eliot (Mrs. William Greenleaf Eliot) written in August of 1895 to a friend, describing her memories of the St. Louis of the late 1830s.

I feel that I am one of the oldest inhabitants now, so few remaining of those who were here with me in 1837.

I left Washington City in September of that year a bride of twenty, very inexperienced but quite wide awake as to my future home and husband's prospects as a missionary.

The steam cars had been running only a few weeks between Washington and Philadelphia. After having been shaken nearly to pieces we left Philadelphia in a steamer and slept that night in New York City. After breakfast started away on the Erie Canal for Buffalo. Slept at Buffalo and went to Niagara and passed two days there, returned to Buffalo and took a steamer for Cleveland. There we took canal again expecting to go on to Columbus, but about the middle of the state at a small town, Hebron, the canal was broken and we were obliged to take a very old broken down stage coach driven by a colored man, quite old too, and there were nine of us packed in; four strangers. Fortunately our own party filled five of the seats. It was beginning to rain and the night was dark. Every little while we were ordered to get out so the stage could be pulled out of what the old man called a "chuck hole" — a small pond of muddy water. We rode all night and arrived at Cincinnati in time to catch a steamer just pulling out for St. Louis. The river was very low and full of sand bars. A poor prospect of reaching St. Louis in a hurry. In a few days we nearly ran out of provisions, and had quite an exciting time getting anything to eat. Our stewart went on shore when the boat stopped to "wood" and caught a large pig in his arms and brought it on board, the pig squealing so every passenger jumped out of his berth to see what could be the matter. The creature was killed and I was told a part of him came on our dinner table! We were reduced to crackers or heavy biscuits and they were stale and poorly kept in the pantry. However, we were young and strong and full of hope.

We arrived, after a two week trip on the rivers, on the third of October and although I had been told much about the smoke and mud, I found it even worse than I imagined. My good friends Mr. and Mrs. Rhodes who were from Newport and had lived in St. Louis several years and who traveled with us kindly took us to live with them on the corner of Market and Seventh streets; so in a short time we were made comfortable. Mrs. B. Allen lived one block east of us and was one of the first to call on me. Mrs. I. Hough, Mrs. Doane (Parker), Mrs. Callender, Mrs. Underwood and about a dozen other neighbors, all so kind and hospitable. Indeed we were most warmly welcomed by Mrs. Rhodes' friends who were nearly all Episcopalians, Mr. P. Choteau lived opposite and old Mr. Lucas then quite infirm, close by us. There were, besides the house Mr. Lucas was in, no houses west of us except a few farm houses. No pavement and a very dusty road, never sprinkled. The woods very thick and Choteau Pond almost surrounded by shanties where the poor gathered so as to use the water for washing clothes. Chills and fever every where, and scarcely a poor family I ever saw but had some one in bed sick — no sewerage — no dry cellars, no nurses, no street cars; but two Hotels and no good boarding places — as a better class of people were coming, each family who came with letters from friends were taken in as we were by them and kindly cared for.

There were only colored servants and they were generally ignorant, but good natured. The markets were good enough for any one and we lived well upon what would now be considered fabulous prices. I think it was in 1840 we moved into our own home on Eighth near Olive. Then on the outskirts of the town and we in our turn took friends to live with us. We had no pavement, only cinder walks and the mud in the streets was fearful! I was fortunate enough in having a good colored cook, and we kept a cow and she pastured around on grass and under woods where the city now is thickly settled. I could then sit at my window and look at the court house with very little to obstruct the view. Visiting among the sick and poor kept us very busy. Public schools just struggling with existence, one or two small dry goods stores, dark streets and muddy ways made life pretty hard for those of us charitably inclined. Policemen few and *very bad boys.*

However matters soon improved and little by little we were encouraged to keep at work and there was a bright side too, for the absence of formality among the inhabitants and the kindness of neighbors in sickness or in trouble of any kind made us seem almost as one family. The family physician, as there were no specialists, was almost as much beloved as the good Pastor. Our table always well supplied because of low prices and great abundance of game and fruit etc. and always of the best quality brought to the door and almost given away, made it easy to keep house. When I think of how easily we could always ask a friend at *any time* to take a meal with us I mourn over the change a big city brings! Perhaps it ought not to be so, but so it is.

I ought to speak of our friends who warmly welcomed us, Gen. and Mrs. Ashley who lived near the great mound, their home overlooking the river, a lovely place and as we had seen them frequently at my father's house in Washington we were glad to meet again in our new home. The Benton family also and Col. and Mrs. Gantt, all old Washington friends, Mrs. Gantt and Mrs. Fremont my old school mates — Sen. Bates also.

There was but one good dress maker. She went around from house to house, a remarkable woman, a strong Unitarian, who talked as rapidly as she sewed and whom many a St. Louis woman blessed for her excellent qualities and warm-hearted excellence. "Aunt Mary Cleveland" she was called by every one. She would cut and fit, rarely staying in any family long enough to finish off any thing.

APPENDIX B
"CHRIST AND LIBERTY"

The Conference Sermon, delivered by the Rev. William Greenleaf Eliot, D.D., on the evening before the formal meeting of National Unitarian Conference, and delivered in the Church of the Messiah, New York City, on October 18, 1870.

"The Liberty wherewith Christ hath made us free." — GAL. v. 1.

My subject this evening may be briefly expressed: CHRIST AND LIBERTY: The Gospel and the freedom of the Gospel; and the text which will chiefly guide us is from the fifth chapter of St. Paul's Epistle to the Galatians, the first verse: "Stand fast therefore in the liberty wherewith Christ hath made us free, and be not entangled again with the yoke of bondage."

Steadfast in freedom, and in the freedom which Christ gives. Not wavering. Not driven to and fro by every wind of doctrine. Not using our liberty as if it were exemption from law, but rather as the free submission to the law of God.

We are glad of that word *stand* fast. It is always a great word with the freedom-loving Apostle; as when he speaks to those who are armed with all the weapons of spiritual warfare — with the sword of the spirit, and the shield of faith, and the helmet of salvation, that they may fight against the powers of darkness and sin — he exhorts them, having done all to stand. Words of sober, thoughtful Christian enthusiasm, which we, in this freedom-loving age, so much need to consider and obey.

What was the liberty of which he spoke? What was the bondage from which we are delivered?

It was the bondage of rituals and forms and ceremonies; of superstition and degrading fear; of human authority and traditional faith and priestly dominion. It was the liberty of spiritual life. The liberty of love which casteth out fear. The liberty of individual thought and action, responsible to God alone. That is the bondage from which we have escaped. That is the glorious liberty of the sons of God, which is brought to us by the Lord Jesus Christ.

It is an excellent heritage which we have received from our fathers, unimpaired, as it came from the great Giver, the inestimable value of which we but imperfectly discern. As with the air we breathe, the preciousness of which we do not know until we come to some pestilential region where disease and weakness enter with every breath — we do not know the comfort and peace and joy in the Holy Ghost which our Christ-given freedom confers, until we are brought to witness the blighting influence of a corrupt and corrupting ecclesiasticism, which binds heavy burdens and grievous to be borne, and lays them on men's shoulders, and uses the fear of hell as the hangman's whip, and converts God's infinite love into vindictive hatred, and builds inquisitions for prevention of free thought, and prisons for its punishment.

It is our heritage, and men never know the value of what they inherit, as of that for which they have toiled and suffered. They do not know its value, and it is equally true that they seldom know its rightful use. They waste it, or pamper themselves with it, or make it a matter of boasting and pride; and escaping from the hardship which alone secures vigor and strength, they become imbecile and insignificant, and that which was conferred as a benediction is changed into a curse.

Freedom is opportunity. It is not so much an absolute good as the opportunity of obtaining what is good. It is deliverance from evil, but itself becomes evil when wrongly used. The chains fall from the emancipated slave, and he rises up a man; but until he has learned to put restraint upon himself, and subject himself to laws more strict and searching than the severest tyranny ever imposed, his manhood needs to be under tutelage as if he were a child. Only when he has learned the stricter rule of manliness, and has substituted voluntary service for enforced obedience, has he fully learned what the gift of freedom means. In like manner spiritual freedom is opportunity of self-direction and self-control under the law of God, and only when wisely used to this end can it insure spiritual growth. It is therefore the strictest and holiest law, the most exacting and impossible of evasion. When seeking to bring us under the severest code of all, the Apostle says, "So speak ye and so do as those who shall be judged by the law of liberty."

The tendency is always to extremes. In the escape from bondage we are always in danger of becoming lawless, and with what is evil too often throw away the good. Thus the gospel frees us from the bondage of forms and rituals. I will have mercy and not sacrifice. The Sabbath is made for man, not man for the Sabbath. First, make clean the inside of the cup and platter, that the outside may be clean also.

It is wonderful what a hold ritualism can obtain over the human mind, and how it gradually takes the place of religion itself. In proof of this we need not go back to the times of Jewish tradition when Jesus spoke, for evidences enough are left at the present day. There are yet found Christian churches where times and seasons, fasts and festivals, forms and ceremonies, are made to bury practical religion out of sight, and those who dare to disregard them, and appeal to the spirit against the letter, are counted no better than infidels. But from all such beggarly elements Christ frees us, and declares that in themselves they are worthless, and, if regarded only for themselves, pernicious. Two outward forms alone are left, with his sanction, both symbolic — Baptism and the Lord's Supper; and even of these, simple and expressive as they are, it is contended that we can find no clear and absolute command for their perpetuity. After reducing the ritual of religion to its lowest point, establishing a minimum of forms below which it would seem that nothing remains, the manner of their observance, and their observance itself, are left to the individual conscience and reason of the believer. "Let every man be fully persuaded in his own mind. He that regardeth the day, regardeth it to the Lord, and he that regardeth not the day, to the Lord he doth not regard it." The priesthood, the Sabbath, the modes of public worship, and everything that belongs to church establishment, whether Catholic or Protestant, depend for their continuance, not on the express command of Christ and his Apostles, but upon their example and the early usage of the church, and the practical ends to be obtained. The essential spirit of our religion and the full sanctity of Christian life can be retained, and have been retained, when all external aids and expressions have been rejected. Of this the Society of Friends has given proof.

But although "all things are thus lawful, all things are not expedient." Common-sense and experience and the teaching of history combine to place restraint upon this liberty, and the danger of rejecting all forms, because they are subordinate to the substance, is proved just as often as the experiment is tried. The Friends discarded the Christian usages, but the necessity of the case compelled them, unawares, to adopt or grow into others of their own; and by their peculiar language and dress, and social and religious customs, they became, even in their attempt at perfect spirituality, formalists above the rest; and in modern times, wherever they have put off their conventionalities, and fallen into the world's ways, they have uniformly and rapidly been absorbed into other churches, so that, as a denomination, they are in danger of passing away. So indispensable is it, practically speaking, to have some outward help, some visible landmarks, some form of expression, by which the faith that is in us can be made known and cherished.

To some extent, and always with similar result, we Unitarians have tried the experiment, and by neglect of the few remaining forms of Christian organization many of our churches have been enfeebled, and not a few of them closed. Wherever we have sought to reduce the ritual of Christianity below that which Christ and his Apostles felt incumbent upon themselves, we have dwindled and languished. I believe that reason and the just exercise of Christian liberty would bring us back, not to superstitious regard of forms, but to their careful observance as needful helps and guides. The baptism of the young, by which they are brought, through outward form, into the visible Christian fold, and made to feel that from the first they are consecrated to God and his service; their confirmation, at suitable age and after fitting instruction in the Christian faith, by which they are placed in just relation to Christ's church, before the world has spoiled and corrupted them; and the more deliberate and mature confession of faith in Christ which the communion service implies; these things, considered as means to a spiritual end, should be more carefully regarded, and placed among our positive duties, under the law of liberty. They are the school-master to bring us to Christ; and we might as well close our schools by saying that education, not schools, is what we want, as to discard religious instrumentalities in the church and conference and prayer-meeting, and at the altar, because religion is what we desire. In other things practical men do not discard the use of means in seeking for the end. But in religion, practical good sense is set aside. If we neglect the means of grace, our spiritual interests must suffer, and we have no right to be surprised when our churches fade, and our children stray from us, and our young men leave the places of their elders vacant. It is only the natural result of the abuse of spiritual freedom which we have not had the grace and wisdom rightly to use.

In like manner the gospel frees us from superstitious fears. We learn from it to respect our human nature, and to look up to God as our Father and Friend. We feel sure that both in time and eternity he chastens us as a father chastens his children, and that, when we suffer for our sins, the just and rightful retribution is administered and restrained by parental love. We do not believe in the total depravity of the worst man that ever lived; nor that any individual whom God has ever created can become absolutely and forever hateful to him. The relation between us and God is that of children and parent; and, however much perverted by our sins, can never be absolutely destroyed. The time will never come to any human soul when it may not, if it will, look up to the Almighty God with the prayer, "Our Father which art in heaven." Man was created in the image of God, and it is like blasphemy against God himself to speak of man as some of the creeds of Christendom have ventured to do. One great mission of our Unitarian churches has been, and yet is, to vindicate the goodness of God by freeing man from the theological contempt and the practical self-contempt into which by false doctrine he has been thrown. From superstitious fears, of whatever kind, founded upon the supposed hostility of God to us, and the consequent power of the Prince of Darkness over our souls, we have been most happily set free.

But have we not gone a step too far? Both in our preaching and our prevailing belief have we not forgotten that there is another side to the truth, which needs to be practically considered? That even the kind providence of God has its sterner and severer aspect, and that the same Father who loves us knows how to punish? "Knowing, therefore, the terror of the Lord," said the Apostle, "we persuade men." "It is a fearful thing to fall into the hands of the living God." "Whoso defiles the temple of God," i.e. the human body in which the soul dwells, "him shall God destroy." "Whatsoever a man soweth that shall he also reap; — he that soweth to his flesh shall reap corruption." Words of tremendous significance, but founded upon philosophy and experience not less than Scripture truth! Have we not kept them, and other words like them, too much in obscurity, until we almost shrink from hearing them? When such language is used in our pulpits, it is called "Orthodox preaching," as if out of place. We escape the censure of Burns to fall under that of Pope, and "never mention hell to ears polite." We enlarge upon the dignity and excellence and glory of our human nature, until we can scarcely explain to ourselves the fact that after all we are miserable sinners! that there is not one of us that doeth good, no, not one! that somehow or other we do need a change of heart before we come into the kingdom of God, and that it is only by constant watchfulness and prayer, and the promised help of the Holy Spirit, that we obtain mastery over the flesh, and enter into the freedom of the sons of God. Yet our people know that they are sinners, and need to be addressed as such. They go to church for that purpose. They feel the hold the world has upon them, and desire redemption from it. They are tired of hearing "Peace, peace, when there is no peace," and "The words of one who singeth a pleasant song," when they ought to hear the trumpet voice, "Awaken, thou that sleepest, and arise from the dead, and Christ shall give thee light." There is an earnestness in the Gospel that we do not sufficiently preach. Is it because we do not sufficiently feel it? Look deeper, dear brethren, into the mystery of our human nature, so grand and yet so base, so glorious and yet so vile, so godlike and yet so contemptible! It is the spirit struggling against the flesh, and the flesh against the spirit. "Who shall deliver me from the body of this death? I thank God through Jesus Christ our Lord."

In the third place, we are freed by the gospel of Jesus Christ, from the bondage of human authority. Under him we claim full liberty of thought and action by which we are individually responsible to God alone. It is the Protestant principle of private judgment, which we, as Liberal Christians, have maintained, as we think, more consistently than the majority of other churches. They are, in general, bound by creeds, confessions of faith, articles of belief, which at the best are explanations or interpretations of Scripture, but are made the standard of orthodoxy, the ground of fellowship, the condition of church membership, in the several communions where adopted. In contradistinction from them all, and in accordance with gospel instruction, we accept no human creed as the authorized symbol of Christian belief or test of Christian fellowship; we refuse to let any man, or body of men, whether Pope, or Council, or Synod, or Conference, or any other organization, stand between us and God, to settle points of belief, to bind our consciences, to prescribe our religious duties. Equally we claim no right to prescribe for others, or to condemn them for differing with us. "Who art thou that judgest another man's servant? To his own master he standeth or falleth; yea, he shall be holden up: for God is able to make him stand."

To this law of liberty we have thus far been faithful as a denomination, both in theory and practice; and although from time to time resolutions have been passed at our public meetings explanatory of our religious standing and practical work, it has never been in such a way as to trammel individual freedom, or establish directly or indirectly terms of admission, or conditions of acknowledged fellowship among our churches. The same men by whom such resolutions have been prepared, have afterwards, in some instances, materially changed their views without withdrawing from their connection with us; and others who have at the time contended against the adoption, with widest dissent, still claiming Christian allegiance, have been left undisturbed, perhaps cherished all the more.

From this treatment of religious doctrine and rejection of religious tests has proceeded the most satisfactory mutual forbearance, by which, though greatly differing, we have met as brothers on equal terms. We have also been very severe, and have a right to be, against those who deny us the Christian name because we follow not in the same company with them, and have quoted Christ's own words in their condemnation. Thus we have stood, and have boasted of standing, upon the broad principle of Protestant Unitarian Christian freedom: "Call no man Master on earth." "All ye are brethren." There is probably no point upon which we are so nearly unanimous as upon this, or so little likely to change. I do not know an individual, clergyman or layman, who would not disclaim all desire to change it. Certainly, if we were to depart from it, our glory would depart from us. If I understand it, our special denominational work has been exactly this — to demonstrate the consistency of Christian faith with Christian freedom. If our cardinal doctrine has been the unity of God, our cardinal principle has been the liberty wherewith Christ has set us free. No word of danger makes us start to our feet so quickly as that which threatens a human authority to interfere with this Christian birthright.

But here, also, we have shown the want of practical wisdom, and have permitted the love of freedom to mislead us. We have confounded things which are quite distinct, and, in refusing arbitrary control, have neglected to use the means of safety by the necessary self-instruction and self-restraint. The fear of dogmatic invasion has betrayed us into neglect of essential truth. We have justly said that all the wide differences among Christian sects are consistent with Christian unity, but have unjustly inferred that such differences are unimportant, and devoid of practical results. It does not follow, because all have equal right to judge for themselves, that their decisions are equally good and useful; or that it matters not what a man believes, provided he is sincere. It does matter a great deal. Few things are more important to the man himself than his belief or unbelief. His inward life, his religious character, depends, to a great degree, upon it. It is said that his faith is everything, his belief is nothing; but this, I fear, is one of the borrowed phrases of men who substitute sentimentalism for strong religious conviction. Upon what is faith founded, considered as a pure spiritual act, but upon belief in truths reverently received? How can we have faith in God if we know nothing of him, or in Christ if we have no definite idea who and what he is? True doctrine lies at the basis of true religion. Jesus said, "To this end was I born, and for this cause came I into the world, to bear witness to the truth;" and we who claim to be his ministers may well devote ourselves to the same great work.

Our liberty is too apt to betray us into apathy, which is a very different thing — as different as life from death. When an educated man says he does not care about doctrines, or what a man believes, he stultifies himself. For, consider the subject to which these doctrines apply: The being of God, and his nature and attributes. Is he our friend, or enemy, and what relation does he hold to the human family? Has he revealed himself to us, and if so, when and by whom, and what is the revelation of his will? Has he withdrawn his spiritual presence from us, or does he still work within us to will and to do? Is the soul immortal, or does it die with the bodily organism? Under what spiritual law does it live, now and for eternity? Is the promise of salvation a truth to be trusted, or only a pleasant dream? Can sin be forgiven and the redemption of the soul perfected, or must the sinner forever remain in hopeless misery and guilt? Can we trust in the Bible as a sufficient rule of faith and practice, or must we set it aside as a collection of myths and old wives' fables? These are not questions to which a careless ear should be turned. Upon their answer everything depends in our religious education and spiritual growth. He who scoffs at them or sets them aside, proves his shallowness of thought not less than his weakness of faith.

We need greater simplicity and directness in our inculcation of Christian truth. There is no denomination of Christians so imperfectly informed as to its prevailing belief as our own. In our pulpits and Sunday-schools too little instruction is given upon the truths of religion, on which, however, its morality must rest. Vagueness of belief therefore prevails, and scepticism of all truth is too often the natural result; and here we find another explanation why our young people leave us for other churches, and why our denominational increase is so slow. Greater definiteness of belief is needed to hold our own, or to attract others. At present there are comparatively few of our laity, especially of the young, who have grown up in our churches, who can give a reason for the faith that is in them, or a fair statement of the faith itself. Our pulpits say very little upon the subject, and when they speak it is to say that what one believes is nothing, what one is is everything. But closer scrutiny will show that when time enough is given for the fair experiment, what one believes makes him what he is, and that the rejection of religious truth paves the way for the loss of religious life. Our churches and our families crave and pine for religious education. We shall perish unless we have more of it.

For such reasons we look with favor upon every effort, however crude, in this direction. We should have proper catechisms, both for younger and older children, to teach the distinctive doctrines of our Christian faith in the Sunday-schools, and carefully prepared courses of instruction for young men and women. Nor can I see the force of the objections so fiercely made against Statements and Confessions of Faith — call them Creeds if you will — as helps in the education of our churches, and for the diffusion of our doctrines. Not as a "campaign document," nor as an authoritative test of Unitarian orthodoxy, nor as a means of conciliating those who have made up their minds to think evil of us, do what we may; but for our own guidance and support, and that our light, if we have any, may be put in a candlestick to give light to the household, and not hidden, as if we were ashamed of it, where it cannot be seen. Every separate church might well have such a Statement of Faith, sufficiently minute for the purposes of practical instruction, and although there would be many shades of difference among them, they would come much nearer to agreement than is generally supposed. Every local Conference might work to the same end, and by harmonizing differences without prejudice to the Christian idea, would bind our churches at once more closely to each other and to Jesus Christ. Even in more general assemblages we might find some method of similar action, if we could only get together in the spirit of love and Christian brotherhood, instead of criticism and recrimination, to learn and declare the truth as it is in Jesus. We are sure that it could be done in some way that would not involve the objectionable features of creed-making, and yet give us the advantage of greater explicitness and frankness in all our work. After all hesitation so natural to a Unitarian on such a subject, I can almost agree with your eloquent preacher of the last Conference (Dr. Bellows), "that there is no duty more urgent than the duty of furnishing our people with a definite Christian Statement of Faith." But in saying this, neither he nor I would forget the limitations. As a denomination we cannot "change our base," or forfeit our birthright of freedom. When it comes to the test of Christian fellowship, we can go no further than the words of him whom we follow, "This is life eternal, to know thee, the only true God, and Jesus Christ whom thou hast sent."

In these three respects, then, it appears that by the rules of Protestant interpretation Christ sets us free: 1. From ritualistic religion; 2. From superstitious fears; 3. From human authority; and in each of them we also learn that common sense, experience, expediency, the usage of the Christian Church, the example and commands of Christ himself, must control us in the use of freedom. The liberty is therefore not license, even when most unreservedly given; not freedom from wholesome restraint, but the opportunity to exercise a larger and nobler manhood in the service of God by the attainment of personal spiritual life.

But there is still something more and deeper that remains to be said, for we are speaking not of liberty in the abstract — if such a phrase can be allowed — but of the liberty which we claim as Christian believers, and which does not seek to throw off its allegiance to Jesus Christ. If there are those who deny that allegiance, they would take but little interest in what I have said, or have yet to say. But addressing a Christian Conference of those who, by the first words of their organization, recognize their "obligation as disciples of the Lord Jesus Christ to prove their faith by self-denial, and by the devotion of their lives and possessions to the service of God, and the building up the Kingdom of his Son," I can speak with confidence upon this point, as one which has been already settled beyond dispute. Yet it may be well for us to be reminded of the explicitness and frequency with which this allegiance to Jesus Christ as the Head of the Church is asserted and claimed. For it is sometimes necessary to go back to first principles, the obviousness of which may cause them to be overlooked.

The quiet dignity with which Jesus Christ assumed his place as Leader and authorized Teacher is not less remarkable than his gentleness and humility. In the Sermon on the Mount, which declares the principles of the new dispensation, we hear the tone of a law-giver who expects to be obeyed: "It hath been said — but I say unto you." He sets aside the whole ritual law of Moses to bring it to a higher spiritual fulfilment. He declares the will of God as one who knows it, and requires men to receive and obey it as his commands. When the sorrowful and sinful are before him, he not only gives them words of sympathy, but invites them to himself as the great Consoler — "Come unto me, ye that labor and are heavy laden, and I will give you rest." When the young man came to him for the way to eternal life, he not only counselled him to obey the Commandments, and to sell all he had and give to the poor, but said, also: "Come and follow me." When his disciples disputed about precedence, he said: "Call no man master on earth, for One is your Master, and all ye are brethren." To believe in him and obey him was made by himself the test of Christian discipleship. He called himself the Way, the Truth and the Life, the door by which men must enter into the fold, the vine of which his disciples are the branches, the light of the world, the living fountain where we can quench our spiritual thirst, the anointed messenger and the beloved Son of God.

The ingenuity of criticism may reject or explain away his words, as reported in the Gospels here and there, but his claims to our allegiance, and his assertion of authority to teach, with power to save, pervade the whole Scriptures and underlie its instructions, so that nothing short of its total rejection, as having no historical basis, can place Jesus in any other light. "Ye call me Master and Lord, and ye say well, for so I am."

Still more explicitly, if possible, and as the burden of all their preaching, did the early disciples speak. Throughout the "Acts" of the Apostles, and in their letters to the churches, the one great aim in view was to preach Jesus Christ as the Leader and Redeemer, the Captain of our salvation, the Author and finisher of our faith. We may say, if we wish to reject their verdict, that they were mistaken, and all wrong, but we cannot question the fact that they so preached Jesus Christ, and him crucified. Whenever the apostles speak of the liberty wherewith Christ has set us free, and of the glorious liberty of the Sons of God, it is the liberty which belongs to the obedient and loyal followers of the Lord Jesus Christ.

"Why then call it freedom, if it is under a master and a King? Why not call it Christian subservience, or anything else rather than freedom, which implies self-direction and control?" For the same reason that the Psalmist said, in words which only those can understand who have learned the lesson of self-command, "I have walked at liberty because I have kept thy law." The teaching of Jesus Christ is the truth of God, and his commands are the law of God, and our spiritual freedom is then most perfectly attained when we have most fully received his truth and law into our hearts. As he himself said, "If ye abide in my words ye shall be my disciples indeed, and ye shall know the truth, and the truth shall make you free."

There are two conceivable ways by which men may come to the knowledge of the highest spiritual truth and to a perfect system of morality. One may be called, for distinction, the rational or philosophical; the other is the path of Christian obedience. By the former a few persons of studious minds and with opportunity for self-scrutiny and metaphysical thought may rise from step to step, seeking after God if haply they may find Him, until at last they come to the highest that man can know, and find it to be the same which Jesus taught to the Samaritan woman eighteen hundred years ago: "God is a Spirit, and they that worship Him must worship Him in spirit and in truth." Or, in seeking to attain the perfect ideal of human virtue, we determine to live every day up to our highest convictions of duty, to do no wrong, to indulge no impure thought, to have no selfish motive, to make the best of every faculty, and control every tendency of evil. Slowly and painfully we struggle upwards, with many doubts and fears, questioning of the way and with uncertain aim, until, having labored long and hard, we come, perhaps, to one who "opens the Scriptures," and shows us, in Christ's example and the gospel system of morality, the rule by which we have unwittingly been striving to live.

To the vast majority of men, and to the young universally, the plainer path of Christian obedience is the safer way. Others must judge for themselves; but for myself I am ready to avow my need of a guide and Saviour. By voluntary and hearty submission to Jesus Christ, we are not humbled, but exalted; not brought under a law of bondage, but under the law of liberty, which is perfect freedom. "I am not ashamed of the gospel of Christ, for it is the power of God unto salvation to every one who believes."

It is well, therefore, that in the first formation of this Conference of Unitarian Christian Churches, notwithstanding the exaggerated fear of creeds, the clear confession of Christ as the Son of God and Saviour of men was made in our Preamble, and *is thereby implied in all that we do*. If the force of that plain avowal has been impaired by subsequent action, I regret it; and certainly that was not the intention of the Conference in the changes made.

The Ninth Article of the Constitution was, in my opinion, a mistake of liberality, with good intention, but without the desired result. It was intended to express no more than is true in all associated religious bodies, even with those who sign the strictest creed — that differences of opinion may exist to whatever extent the honest interpretation of words may allow, and that the proceedings of the Conference, from time to time, are binding only upon the churches that voluntarily consent to them. This had already been expressed, to some extent, by a resolution adopted before the Conference was organized, and it was only desired by the majority of the Conference to emphasize the same principle of congregational independence by incorporating the substance of the resolution into the Constitution itself. Unfortunately, in the last hurry of action, after a long and excited discussion, the Article was adopted in a form which seems to do a great deal more, and almost to neutralize our platform, making this Conference of Christian Churches as open to those who reject Christ as to those who receive him. If we could take out of the Ninth Article the words "Including the Preamble and Constitution," it would be greatly improved. This would leave our congregational liberty, as members of the Conference, unimpaired, while the Conference itself would remain where it was first placed, upon a distinctive Christian basis — an organization into which none but Christian believers would desire to come. But if this method is impracticable or unwise, perhaps some equally efficacious way may be found of expressing our unshaken purpose to stand where we have alway stood, as Unitarian Christian Churches, as disciples of the Lord Jesus Christ, and "having done all to stand"; for this, most certainly, at all times and in every place, it is our bounden duty to do. As a Conference of Churches, and as members of it, the first and indispensable requisite to Christian success is to place ourselves openly, earnestly and unequivocally on Christian ground. Standing there, we may welcome those who believe more or who believe less to work with us, but we cannot either remould our faith or bring contempt on our Christian allegiance for the sake of working with them. A firm and steady adherence to our proper place, in defence of Christ and liberty, without turning either to the right hand or left, going straight forward to do the work of evangelists, "in the cause of Christian faith and works," is the only rightful course for us to pursue.

It would be a sad mistake to court the favor of those called orthodox by any language but that which most plainly conveys the faith we really hold. We desire their fellowship and affection, but only on equal terms. Still greater would be the mistake and the sin to lower the Christian standard for the sake of attracting those who cannot submit themselves to the gospel claims of Jesus Christ.

It is sometimes thought that the way to reach worldly men, and to commend our preaching, is to meet them half way; to preach doctrines that do not require too much faith, and are not strict enough to arouse their fears. No blunder could be greater than that. Faithfulness to Christ is the way to the sinner's heart. Irreligious men are not attracted by scepticisms and denials, but rather amused or disgusted. In the midst of their sins and neglect of God, they have sense enough to know that the fault is not in Christ's gospel, but in their own waywardness and guilt. If they come to the religious life at all, they ask for a Saviour in whom they can trust.

In one of our Western cities the attempt was made to establish a religious society upon what was called the broadest possible foundation, and a covenant was prepared in which no allusion to God was made. The attention of the clergyman was called to the omission, and he explained it by saying that there were a great many infidels and atheists in the community whom he wished to conciliate!

107

Instead of conciliating them, they laughed him to scorn. Among "philosophers, so called," such refinements and evasions of truth, to use no stronger terms, may answer; and ministers in their studies, who know little of the world's throbbing, suffering heart, may imagine that the speculative difficulties which trouble them are the same which keep men from righteousness and truth. But when we come to the working-day world, neither a religion without God, nor a Christianity without Christ, will do.

This is the final explanation of the discouraging reports from so many of our churches. All over the Western States, where the call for liberal Christianity has been so often heard, little bands of earnest men and women have gathered, with every hope of success, and for a time the cause of Christ and liberty has promised well, but too often it has ended in dullness and decay and death. I could name many instances of this, and more that will soon be added to the list. And why? Because neither gospel preaching nor Christian institutions have been the agency employed. Dispensing with the Christian ordinances, with prayer-meetings and Bible instructions to the young, speaking of Jesus Christ as seldom as possible, and never, by any chance, calling him Lord or Master, the pulpit has sunk into insignificance, and the pews into emptiness. Young men who had been educated for the Christian ministry, without ever having professed faith in Christ, and unable to profess it, with a fair amount of talent, with a general good purpose, and with a vague impression that the whole community would be anxiously waiting to hear their gospel of deliverance, have come to those Western outposts with great expectations, to leave them with great chagrin. And why? Because they have had nothing to say of their own which was permanently worth hearing, and they could not say "Thus saith the Lord." They have worked bravely from their own brains to spin the spider-web of ethical instruction and metaphysics, until it has proved too weak to hold the attention of their hearers, and then, having no deeper treasury to draw from, have given up in despair, leaving their fields of work not only unimproved, but unfit for subsequent culture, as if the life and heart had been taken from the soil. I have seen it so often that I am heart-sick at the sight. We have had enough of it.

If we would gain Christian success, we must send missionaries who believe in Christ. Send men who love him and would die for him, as their Saviour and friend, and we shall soon see the difference of result. There is something in personal love and allegiance which overpowers all abstractions. When we impersonate religious zeal by "standing up for Jesus," we feel a fervor of self-sacrifice such as he himself manifested, and which no discouragement can repress. Without it, there is no missionary zeal, almost no missionary success. We have erred in this. We refuse the cross and yet expect the crown. Instead of bringing men up to the gospel, we lower the gospel to them, and so dilute its instructions with worldly morality and skeptical philosophy, that those whom we court complain of its weakness, and go elsewhere to hear the needed rebuke and receive the desired strength. We want John the Baptist to preach repentance, and John the Apostle to preach self-consecration and love.

Dear brethren, consider these things. I know nothing of "right wing and left wing," and have lived too far from the strife to feel their flapping, though I have heard the noise. Let my thirty-six years of hard experience entitle me to speak plainly, and my whole testimony will be given in one word. Be faithful to Jesus Christ. Hold fast to freedom, but equally, nay, more earnestly, to our allegiance. Without it we are nothing, and can do nothing, and all our fancied progress and success will prove to be a delusion and a snare. Stand up with Jesus Christ to do his work. Do not say that such words are a "slogan" of religious cant. They are the battle-cry against sin and wrong. They are the heartfelt expression of loyalty to our Leader and Prince.

To our young men especially, whose love of freedom is impatient of authority, whether human or divine, I would earnestly appeal to reconsider their premises, that they may better understand their work and how to do it. Is your object practical usefulness? to redeem men from sin? to bring them to the knowledge and love of God? And can you hope to be sufficient to yourselves in such a work? Compare your actual success with that of men not half as strong in education and knowledge as yourselves. Why are they doing twice as much work? Because they work with stronger and more definite faith. They have an authority to lean upon to which you dare not appeal. There is no use in your going forth as missionaries unless you have a positive and clearly defined religion to teach. Take your Bibles with you, and argue from them as the sufficient rule of faith and practice, if you would hope to make converts or to hold your own. To preach ourselves is the poorest of all preaching. Especially in the stirring and practical West, youthful lucubrations and Hegelian researches are not what men go to church to hear. They want plain preaching, founded upon the word of God.

In this respect our American Unitarian Association has been severely blamed, as lending aid and comfort to those who preach a gospel of their own, and thus as perverting the funds intrusted to its care. Whether or not its officers have laid themselves open to this censure, it is not for me to say. Probably in the exercise of their discretion they have sometimes erred, as which of us has not? I am not here in their defence, but I am sure that many things have been lately said on this subject which had better have been unsaid and unwritten. Unjust and ungenerous words recoil upon those who use them, and we can find no excuse for some words that have been spoken. We can see no good to come from such severity, nor from the equally severe recrimination that has thus been provoked. "Let all bitterness and wrath, and anger and clamor, and evil speaking, be put away from you, with all malice; and be ye kind one to another, tender-hearted, forgiving one another, even as God for Christ's sake hath forgiven you."

The truth is, that the faults found, so far as they exist, lie at the door of the denomination, rather than of the agents who have administered its affairs. Carelessness about Scriptural truth too much prevails, so that when men of positive beliefs are wanted they cannot always be found, and when found are not always wanted. We have been trying the experiment for thirty years past with how little belief Christian ministers, or ministers in Christian pulpits, can get along. Like the famous horse that was reduced to one straw a day, some have come down to very low diet, and the same result has in some cases spiritually, been seen.

Seriously and sadly, we have been drifting away from Christ in many of our churches, and forgetting the old landmarks. Drifting, we say; not deliberately deserting or denying him, though sometimes betrayed even into that extreme. "Who cares for what a man believes?" is freely asked. "What kind of a man is he? That is what we want to know. We are satisfied with Christ's own test, 'by their fruits ye shall know them.'" But did Jesus choose men who rejected him to preach his gospel? If Peter had continued to deny him, and Thomas had refused to believe, would they have been made his apostles? "Not every one who saith unto me, Lord, Lord, shall enter into the kingdom of heaven, but he that doeth the will of my father who is in heaven." Yes; but Jesus was speaking only of the true and false professors of his name, and the test of truth was obedience. We may go yet further, and admit that the unbeliever in Christ who is a good man, is better than the believer who is a bad man; but we want neither one nor the other as gospel ministers. Why can we not use a little logic and common-sense in religious as well as secular affairs? For the want of it, and for want of closer study of the Bible, we have doubtless been drifting away from our proper moorings, and have imagined it was progress when it has been the reverse. It is much easier to go away from the Christian religion than to improve upon it.

I have sometimes thought, "so foolish was I and blind," that this is becoming the settled and determined tendency of our Unitarian body and of this Conference; that the banner upon which "Christ and Liberty" is inscribed is to be pulled down and another set up, on which liberty alone is written. Such thought, whenever it has come, has filled me with grief, for I love the Unitarian Church as I love my own family and home. But loyalty to Christ comes first. Speaking for myself, and I can speak only for myself, however dear to me the associations of the present and past, I could never consent to remain in any church or communion which is ashamed of Jesus Christ and his gospel. The act which strikes that name from the banner would strike my name from the roll. The Christianity without Christ is no Christianity for me. With my convictions of duty I should have no right, and should feel no wish to be the member of any church, however refined and cultivated and liberal, where the name of Jesus Christ is held in doubtful honor, for I believe his words, "He that is ashamed of me, of him will I be ashamed."

But, thank God, we have no abiding fear that the Unitarian body, or any part of it, will take such suicidal course. The love of peace and liberty, or tenderness for the feelings of hesitating and doubting brethren, may at times betray us into weakness or inconsistency, but the heart of the denomination is and will remain true. Its allegiance to Christ has never for a moment been lost, and will be yet more fully vindicated. Let us not be impatient with each other, or with ourselves. This love of liberty is a Christian impulse, and those who have escaped from the house of bondage may be pardoned for exaggerated fears. We must suffer long and be kind, forbearing one another, forgiving one another. Be not too great sticklers about words and phrases. The letter killeth, the spirit giveth life. But in the midst of all charity and tenderness of construction, with absolute unwillingness to encroach upon the rights of others, we must yet deliver our own souls. In some form or other, unequivocally and steadfastly, openly and fearlessly, we must continue to assert ourselves as a Christian Church, built upon the foundation of the apostles and prophets, Jesus Christ himself being the chief corner-stone.

Let us not be discouraged. We have our troubles and internal conflicts. No Church in Christendom is without its own. Look into them more closely, and we shall find that other denominations, even those that make the greatest boast of union, are torn with schisms and disputes. Our Church has its faults, and we speak freely of them without disguise; but, after all, it is a dear mother Church to us, in which we have found and kept Christian freedom and Christian faith. We sometimes hear it said that Unitarians can never become a strong organization. Rebuke every such word. Let us rather heartily unite upon our two acknowledged principles — Christ and liberty, the gospel and the freedom of the gospel — and thus place ourselves in the vanguard of human progress, devoting ourselves, as our Christian profession declares, "to the service of God, and the building up the Kingdom of his Son."

Finally, yet more than all, we have insisted upon allegiance to Jesus Christ, and upon its full and open avowal, not chiefly because it is the doctrinal truth and the only basis on which a Christian church can rightly be built, but because it is also the only standard under which we can successfully resist the encroachments of sin, and establish the principles of Christian civilization. For this reason, chiefly, we Unitarians have done so little in proportion to our means. "One thing thou lackest; come and follow me." Christian faith is the great effective force of Christian philanthrophy, of Christian work. As in our struggle for national life and freedom, the flag of our country, which some called a painted rag, with its stars and stripes, was the rallying cry, and the sight of it made our hearts beat quick, and filled our eyes with tears, and inspired our souls with heroic courage; so, in the harder struggle against the enemies of God and in defence of his truth and righteousness, and for the rescue of the down-trodden and oppressed, the cross of Jesus Christ, which is to some no more than a piece of dead wood, is the standard under which alone we conquer. Let us never desert it! "Be faithful unto death, and thou shalt obtain the crown of everlasting life." Amen.

APPENDIX C
ON AN ELIOT MEMORIAL

In the early 1920s there was consideration of placing a memorial to William Greenleaf Eliot at Washington University. It is not entirely clear how the idea arose, but it seems to have originated with Charles W. Eliot, the famous President of Harvard University, a distant relation, who in November of 1920 wrote to Robert S. Brookings, then Chancellor of Washington University, mentioning William G. Eliot's great service to education and the need for some suitable recognition of it.

In his reply Brookings stated: "None of the buildings which I have erected for the University bear my name, but on the building known as University Hall [and subsequently in fact renamed Brookings Hall] engraved on the stonework over the portal is 'Eliot Seminary,' with date of its founding, I personally wishing to perpetuate his name."

Some of the Eliot family had different opinions about Brookings' intentions. Charlotte C. Eliot (Eliot's daughter-in-law and biographer, the wife of Henry Ware Eliot), who corresponded regularly with President Eliot and others on the memorial project felt that Brookings wished his own name to be associated with the University as "founder." She observed that Eliot's portrait was "tucked away in a small room," while Brooking's "occupies the most conspicuous place in the University buildings."

Charlotte Eliot made suggestions to Charles W. Eliot on the wording of the proposed memorial, but was insistent upon his composing it, citing not only his experience and widely acknowledged expertise at such writing, but also that his doing so would "arouse interest and add dignity to the tablet. It would make more certain the realization of the plan." Obviously, she had her doubts.

But by 1922, it appeared that the plan would be realized, and a Memorial Committee had been established at the University. Around this time the idea was forwarded that Eliot ought to be recognized not or not merely by the University but by the City of St. Louis as well.

Ultimately, two memorials were drafted, one by Charles W. Eliot, intended as the "public" or "city memorial," the other by Charlotte Eliot, intended to be the

"University" memorial. Neither was ever used. Charlotte wrote to Holmes Smith, William G. Eliot's son-in-law and a member of the Memorial Committee, in 1925: "I earnestly desire that Dr. Charles W. Eliot (to say nothing of myself) will live long enough to see its completion." She also expressed her hope that the tablet would be placed in one of the University buildings. "I should advocate the Archway of the Administration Building, but I doubt if the Directors would be willing and perhaps it would not be possible. I fear Mr. Brookings' interest would cease should Dr. Charles W. Eliot die."

Whether or not this was the entire cause, after Charles W. Eliot's death in the summer of 1926, nothing further was done towards a Memorial to William Greenleaf Eliot for nearly 30 years, when the idea was revived by a group of members of the First Unitarian Church. Under the leadership of Mrs. George (Margot) Pieksen, at the time of the University's Centennial, this group placed the small round plaque on the floor under the "Archway of the Administration Building," now Brookings Hall, which constitutes the only public memorial to the founder.

TO THE MEMORY
OF
WILLIAM GREENLEAF ELIOT
1811–1887
UNITARIAN MINISTER
EDUCATOR, PHILANTHROPIST
WHO WITH MEMBERS
OF HIS CONGREGATION FOUNDED
WASHINGTON UNIVERSITY
1ST PRESIDENT – 3RD CHANCELLOR
1953

THOSE WHO COME NEAREST TO TRUTH COME NEAREST TO GOD

Plaque under Brookings Arch, Washington University Campus
(Courtesy First Unitarian Church Archives)